ONLINE DATING FOR WOMEN OVER *40*:

The Hopeful Woman's
10 STEP GUIDE
to Enjoyment and Success

Christie Jordan

BluePoint Press

Orinda, California   www.BluePointPress.com

ONLINE DATING FOR WOMEN OVER 40:
THE HOPEFUL WOMAN'S 10 STEP GUIDE TO
ENJOYMENT AND SUCCESS
Copyright © 2013 by Christie Jordan
Published by BluePoint Press
An Imprint of Lindsay/Barnett Inc.
120 Village Square, Suite 137
Orinda, CA 94563-2502 U.S.A.
www.BluePointPress.com

Edition ISBNs
Softcover: 978-0-9890106-6-5
eBook: 978-0-9890106-8-9
1. Online dating. 2. Dating (Social customs). 3. Love and sex.
4. Coupling. 5. Internet culture. 6. Computer network resources.
I. Title.

Library of Congress Cataloging-in-Publication Data is available upon
request.
Interior Design by Lisa DeSpain, ebookconverting.com

Praise for Online Dating for Women Over 40

"If you want to optimize your dating life, this book is a must-read."
—Shannon Edwards, Theater Producer

"If you read one guide to online dating, make it this one! It's packed with practical advice and how-to wisdom you can use right now to get started."
—Norma Armon, PhD, Communications Executive

"This book can help make a real difference in your quest for a better online dating experience. It's like having a savvy big sister who has put loads of great information into easy-to-digest segments just for you, and it comes along with a measure of warm support."
—Laura Kaufman, Journalist

"The most comprehensive and informative sourcebook about online dating....Expertly organized and chock-full of helpful tips and insights."
—Lianna Clemons, CEO, Beauty Products Company

"Christie Jordan's witty perspective helps women take the plunge into the modern era of online dating. She offers valuable and ingenuous tips, providing the best opportunities for success."
—Valerie Hotz, Nonprofit Executive Director

"With this book you'll learn why setting up a profile is like launching your personal brand. It teaches you how to create your most appealing online presence to attract the kind of visitors you want. Then you get practical strategies and dozens of sample emails to move the connection forward to an enjoyable first meeting."
—Elaine Jackson, Author, Editor

www.HopefulWoman.com

To Hopeful Women Everywhere

who believe they have the power to re-invent their lives.
Your courage, creativity and determination are inspiring!

May each one of you
find the love and happiness you deserve.

CONTENTS

PART TWO
HELPFUL REFERENCE LISTS

Select The Most Promising Men With the 12 Question Score Card, Great First Date Activities and Knowing Your Must-Haves and Deal-Breakers

PART THREE
BONUS CHAPTERS

Straight Talk About Monogamy, Sex, Body Size and Money

INTRODUCTION

This book is packed with practical tips that you can use to improve your Internet dating experience whether you are already online or are just thinking about getting started.

There are more than one million women using U.S. dating sites and most have not had any coaching or professional marketing experience. Some women who have natural marketing talent have been doing just fine, but so many women report that they receive few responses to their profiles or are not attracting the kind of men they hope to meet.

You can improve your experience and results with a little preparation and some expert guidance.

Online Dating for Women Over 40: The Hopeful Woman's 10 Step Guide to Enjoyment and Success will give you a road map for the journey you are about to take. You will find checklists for how to get ready, tips on how to prepare your profile, guidelines and emails to initiate contact and respond to men you meet online, and an innovative method for making your first dates enjoyable so you're not wasting your time.

Most of all, you will get encouragement from someone who has been in your position! Curious, maybe a little nervous, maybe a little unsure about how to set yourself up for the best possible result? I've been there! That was me when I first tried online dating. But I learned what works and what doesn't and, overall, I had a wonderful experience. I also met a marvelous man, but that's another story.

My goal in writing this book is to share how I learned to be successful with my online dating experience so you can have success, too. I define "success" as enjoying the process without anxiety by meeting interesting new men in a safe environment without making stupid or careless mistakes that limit your options.

This book focuses on advice for women over forty.

While women of any age can benefit from tips on how to create a successful and enjoyable online dating experience, the special focus of this book is to help women over forty get started and enjoy themselves.

I know that a book like this is needed because I couldn't find one. I'm an older woman. After my divorce, I made a serious effort to meet someone through online dating. Most of the advice I found was written for younger women in their twenties who were just starting out. Despite the growing numbers of women over forty who are single, there is a glaring lack of material written just for us. We are not college girls looking for hookups. Most of us have already been married, so we have experience blending our lives with a man in a serious relationship. Many of us are mothers, professionals, business owners, or managers with years of responsibility and experience making hard choices. We have navigated careers and/or family life. We want thoughtful advice about online dating that speaks to us as the smart, capable women we are.

Why am I qualified to write a book about online dating?

As I write this, I am just over sixty years old with thirty-five years of experience as a product designer and marketing manager. For most of my career, I was the CEO of an international design company that created, manufactured and launched consumer products. We took innovative ideas and turned them into viable products people would buy to put in their homes.

I know what it means to make something from nothing.

I know what it takes to get attention in a crowded market.

I know what you need to do to get the desired results when you present yourself online.

Launching yourself online is like creating an original product. There is no one like you—you are unique. You have a unique blend of hopes and dreams. You have a unique blend of resources and restrictions. And you have your unique set of deal-breakers for a relationship.

Setting yourself up with an online profile is like creating the packaging and branding for a unique product. You should do it thoughtfully, with some expert guidance. If you are careless, you will get careless results. If you truly hope to have a positive experience, it's worth putting some time and effort into creating your packaging and then deciding what to do with it.

Don't be mystified or feel overwhelmed. We're not talking about launching a global brand here. You can invest a little time preparing, then start at a pace that matches your comfort level. Some of you will want to blast out and go as fast as possible. That's fine. You will find what you need to make that happen in this book. Some of you will want to go more slowly and digest the experience in smaller bites. That's absolutely fine, too.

The most important goal of this book is to help you feel comfortable and offer advice so you can have a positive experience every step of the way.

Now...let's get started.

PART ONE:

10 STEPS TO YOUR
ONLINE DATING SUCCESS

.

STEP 1
GETTING READY

WHY TAKE YOUR CHANCES
WITH ONLINE DATING?

HERE ARE 10 GOOD REASONS TO TRY

Maybe your life is like mine: I have limited chances in my day-to-day life to meet a new man—very limited. This is not to say that good fortune couldn't strike in line at the post office or in the cheese department at my local grocery store, but my chances of meeting a man are much better ONLINE than IN LINE simply because *that's where there are more available men.*

Men who are trying to meet women go to the Internet because they, too, want success and don't want to waste their time with unproductive activities. These days, surveys of dating sites show that most have a balanced enrollment: 50% women, 50% men.

Does it matter if the single women are more active online than men? No!! There are tens of thousands of single men in your age range who have posted their profiles and are hoping to attract a woman. Not all men will be a reasonable "fit" for you but this book will teach you how to sort profiles for successful outcomes, and, hopefully, have fun along the way.

Never tried online dating? Think it's embarrassing? These days, with so many millions of people registered on dating websites, the stigma of going online has virtually disappeared. Sure, ten years ago it was awkward to tell friends that you were looking online. It felt a little desperate and sleazy. The first time I tried meeting men online was in 2002 and I only told my closest friends what I was doing. I felt brave—like this was something that took courage and fortitude. It's different now.

Online dating is a mature industry with over 7,500 dating services globally. It's growing annually. PlentyofFish.com, the largest free dating site, reports 35.5 million registered users as of January 2012. Match.com, the largest monthly-fee dating site, claims an astonishing 75 million paying members since its start in 1995.

Online dating is a robust, growing business that is here to stay. Participation is up across all age groups, but singles over forty are the fastest growing segment. Studies have shown that all traditional means of meeting people to date are declining: friends and family, workplace, church, school or community activities. Thirty years ago, you might be able to count on meeting a man this way. One hundred and thirty years ago, most likely your marriage would have been arranged or, at the very least, approved by your father. And having sex outside of marriage? Perish the thought!! Times change. Online dating is now a permanent part of the twenty-first century social landscape.

For any reader who has never tried putting up a profile, here are 10 reasons why you should integrate online dating into your social life if your goal is to meet a man.

Reason #1: You're working and your free time is limited.

One of the best features of meeting men on the Internet is that you can do it at your convenience, at any time of the day. Still in your pajamas? No problem! Unlike going to a party, it doesn't matter what you wear. In fact, you can probably write most of your profile in less time than it takes to shop for a new dress and shoes and do your hair for an important party.

Too tired at night to go out? Browse online! You can spend entertaining hours reading profiles or just dip in for a quick five-minute review.

Online dating lets you proceed at your own pace. You have control.

Reason #2: You're older and feel uncomfortable about being out in public looking for a man.

The over-fifty age group is one of the fastest growing segments online. I'm older myself, and don't feel comfortable going out to bars or singles' parties. Online, you have complete privacy. You can share your activities with friends and family if you chose—and I suggest that you do—but if you're a bit shy about starting a dating effort, what you chose to reveal is up to you. Again, you have control.

Reason #3: You can present yourself in your best light.

Your profile is a handpicked selection of photographs and statements. It's like building a window display for a store—with you as the designer. You can present what you like best and think will be most likely to attract a like-minded man. Online profiles are like curated collections that you handpick to showcase yourself.

This means, of course, that your choices reveal a lot about you. We'll discuss this more thoroughly in *Step 3: Creating an Appealing Online Profile: Your Personal Brand* and *Step 4: Preparing and Choosing Your Photographs*.

Reason #4: You're on a limited budget. Going out costs money. Access to men online is a bargain in comparison.

Two of the largest and most well-managed dating sites are completely free to use: PlentyofFish.com and OKCupid.com. You can sign up without contracts or monthly fees.

Presumably, your budget already includes daily access to the Internet. After that, you would just need to prepare a good photograph. While I recommend having a professional quality photo or at least professional guidance preparing a photo created specifically for your profile picture, you could do this for free with your cell phone.

Until you actually go out to meet a man, you don't have to spend an extra dime for dozens of entertaining hours with online encounters. Even if you sign up for Match.com or another site with a monthly fee, it's still a bargain compared to going out for the evening to a bar or event.

Reason #5: Information is at your fingertips. You get to check out the man anonymously and decide whether you want to learn more.

Profiles and photographs are enormously revealing. See *Step 5: How to Read and Decode a Man's Profile.* If you contact a man, his response will give you even more information, and you can still maintain your privacy if you choose to not proceed.

Once you have his name, the entire Internet is open to you for research, and I strongly suggest that you learn as much about him as you can. It's entirely normal these days to check out someone you meet online. Match.com says that over 70% of their members research potential dates using Google, Facebook, Twitter and other search engines.

This is a good motivation for you to Google yourself and fix anything that could be embarrassing (clean up that Facebook page!) or finally put up that LinkedIn profile you've been putting off.

See *Step 8: Identity: Tips for Learning His True Identity and When Should You Reveal Yours?*

Reason #6: You have children and want to protect them.

I'm a mother and completely understand the need to protect children from the confusion of seeing mommy with different men. Only you can decide when it's appropriate to tell your children that you are dating, and, of course, only you can decide that all-important moment when your children are introduced to a new man.

In my opinion, nothing is more important than keeping your children safe. There is no question in my mind that _any_ kind of dating is a risky activity for them. At the very least, you may be rejected, feel blue and find it hard to be cheerful. And, we can all certainly imagine the worst.

As a parent, I personally felt safer with the online dating process than I did meeting strange men in other impersonal settings. Some of us are lucky and have friends or workplaces where we can meet men whose backgrounds are known. For the rest of us, we have to make our own way. Finding men over the Internet was fun and productive for me as a mother with responsibilities at home. I felt hopeful and enthusiastic about my social life while working actively to protect my children. I committed to not meeting a man face-to-face until I had researched his background and knew a lot about him. I hope that you make this commitment, too.

Reason #7: You live in the suburbs. Commuting to a singles' event takes time, commitment and money for fuel. Moving your dating efforts forward while in the comfort of your own home is more efficient than driving around.

You can get discouraged very fast after getting dressed, driving thirty or more minutes to a gathering, paying to park the car and then standing around with no tangible results in meeting a promising man. You're probably like me: generally, the effort I put into an activity defines my expectation of the results: Big Effort equals Big Expected Results. Making a big effort then coming away empty-handed was disheartening.

The worst for me was the lonely drive home.

More often than not, to avoid that lonely drive, I would go to the destination with a girlfriend. It was comforting to have a companion at my side to walk through the door into a room full of strangers, but it also meant that we could choose to spend our time chatting with each other and not spend our time mingling around the room freely. I'm not a world-class mingler. Nor am I a stunningly attractive woman who can just stand there while the men queue up for my attention. To meet people in a crowd, I need to take the initiative.

If you, too, feel a little shy about talking to a new man in person, you will love the comfort and convenience of online dating. It can be easier to take the initiative and introduce yourself online than going up to a stranger and putting out your hand.

Reason #8: You live in a small town and you are worried that the choice of local men is so limited.

This is a really legitimate concern, especially if your small town is somewhat isolated. Let's define "isolated" as driving for an hour without reaching a major population center.

Where I live is technically a small town but it's part of the San Francisco Bay Area, so actually, the population of my whole accessible area is 5 million people. Living in the suburbs isn't as isolating as living in a really small town in a rural setting because within sixty minutes of driving I can get almost anywhere. (OK, make that ninety minutes or more with our horrible traffic.)

If you are a long way from a major population center and are prepared to travel to meet a new man, then online dating is the most efficient and effective way to learn about your prospects.

Or, you might be surprised to learn that there are available men in other small towns near yours. You may or may not know people in the next county, but these days, those isolated men are just as frustrated with their few local prospects as you are.

They are online. Looking for you.

Reason #9: You're shy and feel awkward at parties. You're much better with one-on-one conversation.

This is the VERY BEST part about online dating: all your conversations are one-on-one.

Do you love to "hold forth" at parties and perform for a crowd? Most of us can't do that. I am best with quiet conversations with someone who is listening carefully. I listen carefully. With online dating, you can be quiet and careful about selecting your prospects and thoughtful about responding without the distractions of being in a crowd.

Reason #10: You know what you'd like your future to be. Targeting your efforts to men who share your values and goals is easier and more efficient online.

You can write a profile with a positive tone that will eliminate inappropriate men, or at least most of them.

It's a mistake to think that you have to appeal to the broadest possible audience. If you are athletic, do you seriously want a man who is out of shape? If you are religious, would falling in love with an atheist be awkward for you? What if you don't want children or you love living in the city?

Online profiles can describe your lifestyle and your goals without being bitchy about what you don't want.

People with different backgrounds fall in love with each other every day and can find excitement and harmony embracing their cultural differences, but psychologists who study couples and attraction have found that long-term relationships are best achieved by men and women whose habits are harmonious and who share common values and goals. By sorting through mens' profiles and carefully composing yours, you have the power to pre-select compatible partners.

UNDERSTANDING YOUR GOALS AND DEAL-BREAKERS

Knowing what you want to accomplish is the key to your success. Everything else is just putting in the work and effort. And a little bit of good luck helps! But, if you aren't crystal clear about what your ultimate goal is, it will be harder to create online materials and move effectively towards getting what you want.

An online dating profile is a communications campaign. You will be creating an advertising campaign for yourself—and this book can show you how to do it. It's not hard, but if you haven't been trained in marketing and communications, you may need some tips on how to present yourself. This is similar to creating a brand. *You* are the product!

Your online profile is your statement about your personal brand.

The first step in presenting yourself well online is to consider what you really want and whom you really want to attract. Who is your target audience? Saying that you "want to meet a man and fall in love" is too vague. You need to think in more concrete terms about what you want to do together with your lives.

Let's work on being specific about what you hope to achieve with online dating.

We'll start by recognizing that most guides about dating assume that you want to meet a man, fall in love and get married. I don't make that assumption. Some women just want to find a terrific guy to spend regular weekends with. Some women want even less commitment and hope to find a man to have sex with occasionally.

In the four times in my life that I've used dating sites (two online and two earlier print personal ads) my goals were different each time. Because I was focused, I was successful in finding a man who could help me reach those goals every time. You can be successful, too!

Here are examples of 5 clearly defined goals. Does one of them ring true for you?

- I want to meet a man and be in a romantic love relationship and live together. We'll see how our relationship evolves. I don't have specific plans right now about what happens after we move in together.

- I want to meet a man and fall in a romantic love relationship with frequent companionship but not live together. I like having my own place and don't want to give it up. We should have similar schedules (ex: being available on weekends) and be able to enjoy occasional vacations together.

- I want to meet a man and be in a romantic love relationship, live together and start or blend a family with him. Marriage is mandatory.

- I want to meet a man and be in a romantic love relationship, live together and start or blend a family with him. Marriage is optional.

- I want to meet several men and enjoy a variety of companionship with or without sex.

There are some important conditions to consider adding. This is just a partial list:

- Financial stability is important to me.

- Excessive drinking and drug use is important for me to avoid.

- I am open (or not open) to being a stepmother.

- Practicing a healthy lifestyle of regular exercise and healthy eating is important (or not important) to me.

- Being curious about the world and valuing life-long education is important (or not important) to me.

- Religious or ethnic compatibility is important (or not important) to me.

- Political compatibility is important (or not important) to me.

- I have allergies, sensitivities or phobias (or he does) that restrict activities. Example: animals, food, sunlight, fear of flying.

- I have passions or hobbies that cannot be interrupted. (Or he has.) Example: I've dated two men with restrictive hobbies. One owned a sailboat and wanted to spend every weekend either sailing or working on the boat. The other owned multiple small planes and insisted on spending every weekend flying. As it turned out, I was happy to participate, but their weekend plans were non-negotiable.

- I want to be an equal partner in making all decisions that affect my life. Or: I feel comfortable being told what to do most of the time. Or: some areas are mine and my decisions should be respected. Some areas are his and I will support him whatever he decides.

Does this seem like too many things to think about? Don't despair!! Just remember that there are MILLIONS of available men out there. And, if you think globally, beyond the US borders, even more millions. Many, many millions of men are online and you only need to find a few who share your goals. The odds are in your favor!

The perils of not being clear about your goals

This is not a book about relationships and I don't have any judgments about your choices. And neither should anyone else—*it's your life.* The scope of this book is to teach you a tried and true method of getting to the first date with a man who can help you achieve your goals and live the life you want to live.

The most obvious way to do this is to present yourself in a way that is both truthful and that will also help you *sort out men who will not help you meet your goal.*

This is so important, let me say it again:

Your online profile should not attract men who will distract you from your goal. If the wrong men are inspired to contact you and you pay attention to them, you will waste your time.

Your online profile should be crafted to appeal to a man who will be your partner in achieving your goal. It should also act like a filter and eliminate men who are inappropriate partners for one reason or another. They will waste your precious time.

I know from my own experience being single, lonely and almost desperate for male companionship that I made some lousy choices. Since I'm probably older than you (I was a child in those golden years of the 1950's) I may be part of the last generation of girls raised to believe that we were incomplete unless we were coupled with a man. Single women were still called "spinsters" when I was a kid—a truly horrible label. Women were generally expected to marry by the time they were in their early twenties, then stay at home. My mother got married at twenty-four. I married for the first time at twenty-three. We were carried away with the social norms of our times. Today, most women are so much more clear-sighted and have the insight and courage to make a wider range of choices.

So, again: Make your online dating experience more successful and enjoyable by knowing your goal! In *Step 3: Creating an Appealing Online Profile: Your Personal Brand* we'll talk about how being goal-oriented influences your profile writing and whether or not you should state your goal clearly in your descriptions. For now, it's enough to understand what you really want.

Getting a clear understanding of your lifestyle goals

Maybe you know exactly what kind of lifestyle you'd like to lead. If so, skip this section! Some of the rest of us are less clear. Or, we haven't realized that our lifestyle goals from our twenties and thirties no longer fit very well in our forties, fifties and beyond.

It's worth taking time to consider what kind of lifestyle you want to be leading five years from now.

Here are some tricks you can use to help you visualize and become clear about how you want to live:

- Build a picture board: Tear images from magazines that help you visually define your desired lifestyle. Young professional in the city? Mother in a family house? Older adventurers exploring the world? Musicians playing together? Scholars dedicated to life-long learning? Activists working for social change? Gardeners enjoying your private moments together?

- Go to a therapist or counselor: This is especially important if you've had a traumatic end to your last relationship, or if you keep making the same relationship mistakes over and over with the same disappointing results.

- Look at your friends and extended family: Which couples do you admire? Which couples seem stiff, uncomfortable or even unhappy? What's the difference?

Save yourself some of the heartache born from delusion and DO NOT use couples in motion pictures as your models, especially idealized, romantic ones. Nobody lives their years like the story you've seen in ninety minutes.

You risk being disappointed if you're not clear about what kind of lifestyle you really want. No fantasies now. Richard Gere as the billionaire in *Pretty Woman* is not riding in on his limousine to rescue you from single life! You will create your own destiny by knowing what you want, staying focused and being willing to work to achieve your goal.

Be realistic, put in the effort and enjoy success. If you live in a fantasy world or just hope that your perfect future will be handed to you, you will be disappointed.

Online dating is a communication campaign: Knowing what you intend to communicate is the first step.

For women who want to have children, it is especially important to not waste time dating men who don't want children, are afraid to be a father or already have enough children and don't want more (unless you are fulfilled being a step-mother).

For women who already have children, knowing what you expect from a new man's involvement with your family will help you find a man who shares your goals. You risk disappointment if you aren't clear in your own mind about what you hope for. Do you want another co-parent? Do you need financial support? Are you willing to offer him financial support? Are you up for the challenges and joys of a blended family? Whose well-being comes first when you have to make a choice: your children's or your own?

For women who aren't interested in having children or raising them, is it necessary to find a man who feels the same way? Based on my experience, I would say "yes". Having the responsibility of children in your life is a primary lifestyle condition and can heavily influence your comfort zone. If you are certain that you don't want to have children, try to screen for men who feel the same way. If you are certain that you don't want to spend time trying to do your best with his children, try to screen for men who are not fathers. Just note that if you're dating in your forties and older, you will eliminate a lot of interesting guys by refusing to consider a man who has children. There are a whole lot of divorced guys out there who are trying to be responsible fathers. And...if they're not responsible...do you really want them?

Keep your goals clear and your standards high.

What are your deal-breakers? Deciding how flexible you want to be about your goals is a key part of your online dating success.

Some compromise is inevitable when two people get together. At least it is when two people who have a lot to offer each other get together. If you are a blank slate with nothing going on, then you have nothing to compromise. But—obviously you have a lot to bring to the party—otherwise you wouldn't be reading this book!

Think about what is non-negotiable for you.

What are your deal-breakers?

Here are my five instant deal-breakers:

- **Deal-breaker #1:** I don't like excessive drinking and won't spend my time with someone who drinks a lot. Addictions and lack of self-control are deal-breakers for me.

- **Deal-breaker #2:** I'm active and fit and can't see myself with someone with unhealthy eating habits. A pre-existing condition that needs to be managed is OK with me, but self-destructive life-style habits are not. Being morbidly obese and unwilling to commit to good health is a deal breaker for me.

- **Deal-breaker #3:** I am not religious. I can support someone's religious beliefs but will not be subjected to fundamentalist rules of woman's behavior. Being told that because I am a woman, my future in society must be limited is a deal-breaker for me.

- **Deal-breaker #4:** I am politically and socially progressive. I would like to be open-minded about other points of view but can't agree with oppressive or abusive policies that suppress the rights of others. It doesn't matter about being Democrat or Republican. Being closed minded about social issues and supporting public policy that discriminates is a deal-breaker for me.

- **Deal-breaker #5:** I am educated and curious about the world we live in, and I believe in life-long learning. I love to go out, travel, meet new people, explore new places, read, take classes and stay current with world affairs. Being a couch-potato and wanting to stay home and watch TV is a deal-breaker for me.

Maybe this seems like too much thought before you simply hop online and write a paragraph or two. It could be. It's *possible* that you can just stumble across your perfect mate by popping up a photo and posting a few hopeful sentences. But remember: planning ahead will not only increase your chances of success, it will give you a greater sense of control. You will understand what you are writing and whom you hope to attract.

At the end of the book is a list of potential deal-breakers gathered from my own experience and the experience of my friends. See the chapter *Know Your List of Potential Deal-Breakers.*

Here's an example of recognizing a deal-breaker: my friend, Patty, broke up with her finance because of his uncontrolled road rage. She told me: "He was peaceful and wonderful until he got behind the wheel of a car. Driving with him scared the bejeebers out of me!" His road rage revealed that he couldn't control his anger. Sadly for both of them, he was not willing to consider anger management training.

Listing negative behaviors or situations is not intended to discourage you but rather to give you a roadmap of behaviors to avoid and be alert for when you meet a stranger online.

My mission here is very simple: *To save you time and help you be successful meeting your goals with online dating.*

Learn to "qualify" your "prospects"

It's obvious that by going online you hope to attract men, but who will they be? Once again, we're talking about pitching your profile to the type of man you want and filtering out inappropriate men. In a business setting, we would say that we are "defining our market" and will create materials to appeal to our "target customers." What is less obvious is that our targeting is designed to eliminate inappropriate viewers. *We want to get responses only from people who are genuinely potential "customers."*

If you were selling real estate, you would write appealing advertisements, then you would spend time "qualifying" the people who respond. Are they genuine buyers? Do they have the money to actually buy the property? Are they "looky-loos" or "tire-kickers"—to borrow phrases from other sales environments. If a real estate agent spends all of her time with people who are just looking, she'd starve to death. She needs to sort through the people who respond to her ads to figure out who is worth her time. To be successful, she needs to focus on the "qualified" buyers who share her goal of selling them real estate.

Sorting through men who respond to your online profile is just like that. You need to spend your time focused on men who share your goals and not waste time on men who will disappoint you. Of course, there are no guarantees here, but sometimes you set *yourself* up for disappointment. If you're willing to put some thought and effort into your online dating, this book will help you to learn how to avoid making this type of mistake.

Don't set yourself up for disappointment. Write your online profile to attract the kind of man you want to spend time with. If your profile attracts fewer responses, that's fine. They will be more "qualified."

Every campaign requires planning to be successful

Your online profile is essentially an advertisement for you—being with you, spending time with you or possibly falling in love with you.

Once you have an understanding of the kind of man you're trying to reach and the lifestyle you hope the two of you will lead, you will be able to choose your pictures and write your profile descriptions with focus and effectiveness.

Be sure to never misrepresent yourself and chose photos and descriptions that are true to the type of life you hope to be leading in the future. You'll find practical guidance on how to do that in *Step 3: Creating an Appealing Online Profile: Your Personal Brand.*

SETTING UP AN EMAIL AND TELEPHONE NUMBER THAT ARE DEDICATED TO YOUR ONLINE DATING

Before you sign up with an online dating site, you should consider how men are going to contact you. Will you use your existing personal email? Will you give out your existing cell phone number?

If your life is like mine, both of these are vital to your everyday life and your ability to stay connected with friends and family. If you have to block either your email or cell phone number, it would be an unwelcome hassle. While the odds are minuscule that you will run across a crank or troublemaker, we have all heard stories about phone stalkers and nasty email problems.

In all my experience with online dating, I NEVER gave out my home telephone number, but I did give out my cell phone number and personal email address. I never had a problem. My friends never had problems. Maybe we were lucky.

It's important that you feel safe and comfortable contacting men online and having them contact you. Being cautious and careful is wise. If you would feel more comfortable building a "firewall" between your true identity and your online dating identity, then you need to consider a dedicated email address and dedicated cell phone number for online dating.

You can do both for very little money. A dedicated email can be completely free. I would recommend doing at least the email. We will discuss a separate telephone number later in the chapter.

Before you register with an online dating site, get a new email address

Set up a new email dedicated exclusively to your online dating correspondence. Using Gmail from Google is a good choice. This email will be separate from your usual personal email address.

You will use this dedicated email to register with online dating sites and receive notifications that you have matches or messages waiting for you. If you and a man wish to exchange emails off the site's message boards, you will use this new dedicated address.

You already have a personal email and probably have an email for work, too. You may be thinking: *"Add another email? This is too much to keep track of!"* Or: *"How am I going to get another email on my smart phone?"*

Here's why you should do this:

- It's free.

- It's a security measure for you. Having a separate dating email means that you add another layer to your privacy.

- If you have the misfortune of giving your email to a weirdo, you can shut down this address without affecting the rest of your life.

- It helps you focus. When you go to this address, everything there will be related to your dating efforts. Your attention will not be bouncing around.

It takes some planning and discipline to schedule checking your dating email. I recommend checking in once a day or every other day. If you check in multiple times during the day like you do with your personal email, the lack of activity may discourage you. Remember, you want the entire dating experience to be positive and enjoyable.

Setting up a new email with a Google Gmail account

Gmail is part of Google. It's free, fast and easy to sign up. There are no contracts or fees. If you can get Google on your computer or smart phone, you can set up a Gmail account.

- Go to www.google.com
- Click the SIGN IN button
- Click on CREATE AN ACCOUNT FOR FREE
- Pick a user name that will be easy for you to remember. Remember, there are MILLIONS of people with Gmail so don't be surprised if your first few user name requests are taken.

Can't get the name you want? Try this trick

Adding four or five numbers to the end of a word or short phrase will help your chances. In fact, the right combination of numbers will guarantee that you get your choice. Just keep it something simple that you can remember. Note that in the examples below, I just run across the keyboard or repeat a number.

Choose a phrase or word that sounds pleasant and optimistic for your email name.

Here are some examples:

lifeisgood6789
candoitnow9876
inbloom4545
humorhappiness1234
happyhappy7890
birdsonwing3333
flowersong4321
musicharmony2222

Here are some types of phrases to avoid:

hottotrot4you
sexygirl4444
callmeanytime8675
loveschardonay4
cantwait67890
yourtoppick5678
milliondollarbaby4567

Google will ask for your name, birthday, current email address and mobile phone number. They need the mobile phone number for recovery if your email has problems. The reason they want the birthday is to protect children under eighteen years old. Google has the strongest anti-spam and anti-hacking system on the planet, which helped me feel comfortable and secure.

Putting the new email on your smart phone

If you are using Gmail, you can access your new dating Gmail account on your smart phone from the Google search page. If you have another email provider, you may need to go to your phone service office for help.

Maybe you're a very tech savvy person and can figure this out. I'm not and needed help so I went to my cell phone service provider. In my case, this was Verizon. I just went to one of their offices and the helpful customer service person persuaded the phone to receive two mailboxes from different carriers with easy to find icons.

Should you set up a dating-only telephone number?

Are you worried about giving out your telephone number? Would you feel safer if you had a cell phone number dedicated to your online dating project? Not everyone will want to take this step because it does mean extra handling and extra expense. I used my everyday cell phone for online dating and never had a problem, but if you are nervous about this, there are two alternative approaches you can use to create a telephone number that you can cancel at any time.

At the very least NEVER GIVE OUT YOUR HOME LANDLINE TELEPHONE NUMBER.

Telephone services aren't free, of course, but there are two choices that will keep your costs down.

Buy an inexpensive, pre-paid cell phone

AT&T has prepaid phones that start at $19.99 for the phone and $25 for a monthly plan. Both T-Mobile and Best Buy have phones for about $50. All phones will also text. Most have cameras and connect to wireless headsets. T-Mobile has no contracts. You should check with the other companies as their plans and contracts change all the time, but you do not want more than a monthly contract.

You can either prepay a set amount for a prepaid card or sign up for a $25 to $30 a month plan that can be cancelled after any month.

You can find specific information about prepaid phones at: www.att.com, www.t-mobile.com or at www.bestbuy.com.

Pros:

- Protect your every-day cell phone number.

- Add an extra layer of security to your identity.

- If you have any problem with a weirdo, you can cancel this phone number without impacting how you connect with your friends and family.

Cons:

- More equipment to keep charged and keep track of. Ugh!

- Additional expenses. Figure $50-$75 initial outlay then about $20—$30 a month after that. (See section on *How Much Money to Budget for Online Dating.*)

Skype from your computer, smart phone, tablet, or TV

Skype is a communication service that will enable you to call with the option to use video. The app is for any device and is free: www.skype.com

Forty million people have Skype accounts that let you call FREE to anyone with a Skype number. Within the US, you can call any non-Skype telephone number for less than three cents a minute. Usually, I buy a $10 credit on Skype and just draw down on it. This takes me about a year! You can also buy an unlimited US and Canada calling plan for $2.99 a month, but that's probably more than you need for online dating.

Signing up for Skype is free. You will choose a user name and be assigned your own Skype phone number. If, for any reason you decide to discontinue the number, you can delete the account.

Please consider the tips for choosing a user name as outlined above. On Skype, your user name is called "Skype Name", and, as always, your choice will reveal information about you. To keep your life simple, why not use the same name as you have chosen for your new email account?

Pros:

- Skype is a wonderful service that you will want to have anyway, if you don't have it already.

- The cost is minimal.

- Protect your everyday cell phone number. Add an extra layer of security to your identity. If you have any problem with a wierdo, you can cancel this phone number without impacting how you connect with your friends and family.

Cons:

- While you can call out to any number, your Skype number can only receive calls from another Skype account. An ordinary cell phone number cannot call in to you on Skype. So, if you give out your Skype number as your primary contact, you MUST IDENTITY THIS NUMBER AS SKYPE. Hopefully, the man will also have Skype. If not, just tell him to download it free from www.skype.com.

- You may be nervous about appearing on video, and he may be also. Remember that video is an option. You can turn it off.

Moving over to your everyday email and cell phone

Only you can determine your comfort level. As I mentioned earlier, I just used my everyday email address and cell phone number for online dating but I may be older than you. Presumably the men in my age range, which would be fifty to seventy years old, are a better-behaved group than twenty-somethings, but I can't cite a study confirming this.

At some point you will not want to bother with separate emails and cell phones. You will know when you reach that point. Just cancel the services. You can always start again.

WHAT SHOULD YOU DO ABOUT MOBILE APPS?

It's unavoidable that the big growth in communications is with mobile applications on your smart phones and tablets. Analysts who look at the future business models of online dating business estimate that 45% of the traffic going to dating sites is already coming through cell phone mobile apps. The anticipation is that the traffic will only grow. This makes sense, with so many millions of people becoming more comfortable moving many daily functions over to their handheld devices.

So, what should you do? It depends entirely on your comfort level. Every dating site on which you enroll will have a mobile app. You can download it to your phone and access your account this way. The advantage is immediacy and the ability to respond quickly from anywhere if someone contacts you.

For writing your profile and choosing your pictures, it will be easier to work on a screen larger than your cell phone! Do this on your larger computer.

Personally, I prefer to work at my desk so I can keep my calendar and notes organized. Yes, I still like to look at a paper calendar for reference. I do have an online calendar but I haven't mastered the proper buttons on my phone that will let me look at my calendar and an application at the same time. I guess I'm just old fashioned, but I like being physically comfortable and organized which is easier (for me) at my desk.

As this is written, mobile apps are just starting to shift the usage habits of online daters. It's dynamic and moving quickly. You should enjoy experimenting with what's available now while looking forward to the new ways of making online dating even easier and more accessible in the future.

HOW MUCH TIME SHOULD YOU DEDICATE TO MAKING A FAIR EFFORT AT ONLINE DATING?

How much time you put into an online dating effort is, of course, determined by how motivated you are. Also, nothing will inspire you to put in more effort than a taste of success. So, let's take a realistic look at how many hours you should expect to invest in your online dating project to get you to a level where you feel comfortable, confident and prepared to enjoy the process.

Researching dating sites: Two hours should do it

With so many to choose from, how will you know where to start unless you do some research? This might take the form of:

- Browsing the home pages and links on three to four sites. I recommend looking at Match.com, OKCupid, EHarmony and PlentyofFish. If you want to belong to a specific niche like Christian, Jewish, Black or Asian dating sites, look at that, too. More information about dating sites in included in *Step 2: Choosing an Online Dating Service.*

- Talk with your friends about their experience.

- Spend an hour Googling dating site reviews. Please keep in mind that many of the review sites are phony pages set up to look like reviews but are really advertisements to put their site up at the top. Read web pages that claim to be listing the Top Ten Dating Sites with a grain of salt. If you can find personal commentary on yelp.com or a blogger who clearly doesn't have his/her own site, this is better.

Preparing for your profile: Allow three hours minimum

Don't underestimate the amount of time it will take you to sort photographs and write drafts of your profile essays. Plus, acknowledging that it will take some time helps you realize that this is a serious effort worth some serious thought. Your social life and romantic future is worth your investment of time.

Many of us have a hard time finding a three to four hour block of time! If that's you, expect to dip in and out of getting your photos ready. You will read in the chapter *Step 3: Creating an Appealing Online Profile: Your Personal Brand* that you will draft your essays in a word processing program (ex: Microsoft Word) instead of directly onto the site. This makes it easier for you to stop and start as you are putting your profile together.

It's generally advisable to not build your profile on a mobile device. If you have a laptop or computer with a larger screen, spend your time there. Handhelds are create for quick answers, but when you are building a webpage that might be up for months, you would be better off doing it on a larger screen.

Your first week online: Three or four hours or more

It could be like Christmas morning, all those promising contacts waiting for you! Or, your inbox could be thin. Not to worry. You will just need to stir the pot by searching for matches yourself. One way or another, you will probably have a hard time not running to check your inbox multiple times a day.

Try to restrain yourself and check once a day, when you have thirty minutes to review men who have contacted you directly or just viewed your profile. If you can, allow a block of one hour (maybe on the weekend) when you can relax with more time to spend.

Reading a man's profile takes from one to ten minutes depending on how much he has entered.

Answering a man's contact takes from thirty seconds (to click delete) to fifteen minutes to read a serious email from a man with a serious profile and consider what you want to say back.

What happens after the first month is up to you. If you continue to contact men and respond to contacts, with practice you will become faster at answering.

Continued participation online: Two hours per week

Continued participation on each dating site can take as much time as you wish. A realistic time budget is two hours per week, or at least eight hours a month to put in a fair effort. This includes responding to men who have viewed or contacted you and also initiating contact yourself.

And don't forget the time you need for your dates! Even if you meet a man for a brief cup of coffee, you will most likely need time to get ready and travel to the meeting place. Anticipate at least two hours for each date.

Here's a general summary:

Activity: Setting Up Your Profile	Time Needed	Find more details on this page
Researching online dating sites	2-3 hours	45
Setting up dedicated email, phone, etc	2-3 hours	31
Preparing your profile	3-4 hours	39
Your first week online	3-4 hours	40
Continued profile participation time per week	2 hours	41
Activity: Continued Participation Online	Time Needed	Find more details on this page
Continued profile participation time per week	2 hours	41
First dates	2 hours each	157

HOW MUCH MONEY SHOULD YOU BUDGET TO SET UP ONLINE DATING?

You would expect that any worthwhile, life-changing project would have some expenses associated with it. Relatively speaking, online dating is a bargain. You can invest very little money and still have an enormous impact on your life.

Let's take a look at the minimum expenses you can anticipate and also note which other expenses are optional. All of these items have been discussed in detail previously in this chapter or in upcoming chapters.

Activity Options	Cost	Find more details on this page
Dedicated dating email	$0 Free	32
Dedicated dating cell phone	$20—$50 Optional	35
Paid dating site subscription	$19—$30 monthly	45
Free dating site membership	$0 Free	46
Skype account	$10 Credit	36
Professional photography for profile picture	$0—$200 Varies	93
Wardrobe and grooming updates	$250 Varies	142

STEP 2
CHOOSING AN ONLINE DATING SERVICE

Online dating is a big business, generating billions of dollars a year for companies that own dating sites. There are now over 7,500 dating sites globally with millions of members.

In the U.S., our awareness is usually limited to a handful of large, well-publicized sites like Match.com, EHarmony, Yahoo.Match and OKCupid. If you have a particular focus and want to meet men within a specific social, religious or ethnic group, you might also know about the smaller niche sites like JDate, ChristianMingle, BlackPeopleMeet, OurTime or even the vegetarian VeggieRomance.com.

Millions of men and women are turning to online dating to find life partners, activity companions or casual sex. What used to be an activity only practiced by a few early adopters has become standard operating procedure for singles trying to improve their social life.

Singles of all ages are online. It's no longer a wild experiment that you need to be ashamed of trying. If you're single, the question is settled: putting up a profile online is normal, commonplace and even expected. The only experiment is which site to choose, but we'll get to that in a minute.

You need to remember that dating sites are businesses whose success depends on people to signing up as members.

This means that almost everything you see in their advertisements is a sales pitch. Some of what's advertised may, in fact, be true. But you deserve to understand that you are signing up for a business service.

Let's go behind the scenes so you can understand more about your role as a participant. This will help you become an informed consumer.

Going behind the scenes of the dating website business model

Why is online dating such a growing social tool? Why has there been a recent explosion in the numbers of dating websites? Fifteen years ago, Internet dating might have been a daring thing to do. Today, it is mainstream. Dating sites have become a robust segment of the online service industry with business analysts tracking their performance. Any activity that involves millions of Americans is going to draw enormous attention.

The tracking firm Experian Marketing Services reports that 1.6 million single women use online dating sites in a typical month. (For more information and up-to-date numbers, go to www.experian.com and search their public site for articles on online dating.)

Here are six reasons why online dating has become a mainstream social activity:

- Women have entered the workforce in huge numbers and are marrying later. They may be separated from their hometowns, their college towns, their families and more traditional ways of meeting men.

- There are more divorces in the U.S. population.

- Adults are more mobile today and move around the country. Both women and men need to make new friends in their new geographical areas.

- The population is aging. There are just more older singles now.

- Using the Internet has become ubiquitous for everything from shopping to renewing library books to online banking. People have learned to be comfortable going online for a wide variety of daily functions. Email, Facebook, Skype, Pinterest, etc., have made millions of people comfortable with staying in touch with friends on line. Jumping from "staying in touch" to "meeting" isn't such a big leap.

- The promise of a larger selection of people to date is obvious with online dating. As Internet use has matured and more people feel safe, online dating is rapidly expanding to mobile apps for smart phones and tablets. With more outlets, there are more users. This does put some pressure on you to present yourself wisely and be sensible about setting your goals. (See the section on *Understanding Your Goals and Deal-Breakers*.)

These days, it's reported that one in six marriages started with a first date that was initiated through a dating website. As there is no marriage license which requires couples to disclose where they first met, we'll never know if this is really true. But, certainly every year, people meet and fall in love after finding each other online.

THE 4 BASIC TYPES OF DATING SITES

You can divide the available dating websites into four broad types:

Type #1: Paid Membership / General Population: Monthly membership fee to access all services including the ability to email members and receive emails from members. These sites represent the general population of singles without a specific focus on religion, ethnicity or lifestyle commitment. Examples include: Match.com, EHarmony, Chemistry.com.

Paid dating sites often advertise that it is free to sign up as a member. This free feature is very restricted because the free "member" cannot send or receive emails from anyone on the site.

Paid dating sites sometimes include these restricted "members" in their total count of people using the site. This is confusing, since having thousands of "members" who can't contact you and whom you can't contact won't do you any good trying to get dates.

Note that on the free dating sites, every single member will have access to the site's email features. Men may or may not be active on the site but at least they are not "mute members" looking at your profile. This makes the free dating sites' member totals a more reliable indicator of the number of men available for you to contact.

Type #2: Free Membership / General Population: Free to sign up. No monthly fee. All members can send and receive emails. These sites represent the general population of singles without a specific focus on a religion, ethnicity or lifestyle commitment. Examples include: PlentyofFish.com, OKCupid.com.

Type #3: Paid Membership / Niche Population Focus: Monthly membership fee to access all services including being able to email members and receive emails from members. These sites represent a specialized niche of singles by focusing on a specific religion, ethnicity, race or lifestyle commitment. Examples include: JDate.com, ChristianMingle.com, BlackPeopleMeet.com, SeniorPeopleMeet.com.

Type #4: Free Membership / Niche Population Focus: Free to sign up. No monthly fee. All members can send and receive emails. These sites represent a specialized niche of singles by focusing on sexual orientation, relationship expectations or lifestyle commitment. Examples include: Adam4Adam.com, AmorenLinea.com.

Which type is more effective?

You might be curious as to whether free sites or paid sites are more effective in matching people and giving you opportunities for dates. I haven't been able to find any reliable data about this. Personally, I had just as good of an experience on the free OKCupid as I did on the paid Match.com but I'd have to give the edge to OKCupid since that's where I met the wonderful man in my life.

Which type has the more serious members? Common sense would tell you that if someone pays for a service, s/he is more likely to treat it carefully and put more effort into setting up a good profile. This could be true. But when I was online, I only paid serious attention to profiles that showed some real effort and there are plenty of these on both the free and paid sites. Although the free sites OKCupid and PlentyofFish do have a lot of younger members and men who put up nearly empty profiles, I had more than enough opportunities for serious-minded older men on OKCupid to keep me happy.

You should certainly consider one of the niche dating sites if it aligns with your lifestyle or ethnicity. Being part of a specific group can help assure that both of you have shared interests and experiences. This can certainly move your communication forward faster.

Because online dating is such big business, new sites are being launched all the time. For consumers, the new ones will still fit into one of the four groups.

Dating sites for casual sex

Just a quick word about the sites targeting casual sex: Date-Hookup.com is the fifth most popular dating site in the U.S., as of this writing. It's free. It's sexy.

DatingHookup.com is owned by the same company that owns Match.com but on DateHookup.com, the profile pictures tend to be suggestive and the profiles are short and to the point. "Hookup" says it all. On the site's chat room, there are over 9,865,000 posts to their "Sex and Dating Forum," by far the largest number of posts of any of their forums. "Enter at your own risk" says the link.

If you want to have one night stands, this may be your place.

Can a dating site really match you with compatible men?

You've heard claims that sound like magic, but can a dating site really match you with compatible men in their database?

The short answer is "yes." Sites that say they have a method of matching you with compatible mates really do have personality tests and algorithms that sort data and consider hundreds—sometimes thousands—of variable factors. These sites have invested a lot of money in behind-the-scenes research and software to be able to search through their member database, trying to find people who are compatible with you. The major sites that claim to have matching capabilities really do try their best.

How successful are they? So much depends on the self-limiting pool of members. They can only search through the database they have. For this reason, it's probably a good idea to include one very large dating site in your plans. These would be Match.com, OKCupid, PlentyofFish or EHarmony.

Another limitation is how many questions you answer. If you don't give the site your information, they won't know what to do with you. Generally, women will answer more questions than men.

Not all the information the site uses comes from answers to your questions and the statistics in your profile. With today's technology, the sites know where you go on the site and what you do. They track which men you click on and whether you contact them or respond to their contacts. Your behavior on the site is called "revealed preference" and it's an important factor in their matching process. So, if you say that you want to date tall, Buddhist vegetarians who live nearby but you keep contacting short, Christian meat-eaters who live fifty miles away, the algorithms will learn this and factor your actual preferences into your compatibility searches.

Don't get too jumpy about a website knowing your every move. That's just today's reality on the web. Tracking your clicks is something that every major website does—from Amazon to L.L.Bean to Travelocity to Google. They all pay attention to what their customers do.

So, in essence, you are a customer in the Internet dating world. You are wanted, deeply wanted, by these businesses. They are highly motivated to keep you happy and are constantly tweaking their websites to give you a better user experience.

Dating sites are trying powerfully to attract you and, like all salespeople, it's only the promise of the most glorious experience that is presented on their home pages and marketing materials. Ultimately, you must be responsible for your own experience and be proactive on a dating site. Do not just take a passive position by putting up a careless profile, then waiting for their search engines to do all the work for you. The capabilities of the site's search engines can help, but it's what you bring to the party that will determine the quality of your experience.

The privacy of your data and preferences

Yes, I'm jumpy about my information being distributed without my knowledge, except that by agreeing to go online and enroll on a dating site, I have agreed to allow the site the use of any information I've provided. Hopefully, all personally identifiable information (name, email, phone number, credit card) has been stripped out by the time the millions of data points are aggregated so that my privacy is protected. I have no reason to believe otherwise, since the value in a large database lies in the behavior patterns of large numbers of people, not just in my little choices.

Databases and customer metrics are valuable assets for a dating company. The scale of raw data about human mating behavior gathered by these dating sites is unprecedented. If OKCupid has nearly 300,000 questions and millions of members are answering even a small fraction of them, you can easily see that hundreds of millions of answers makes a massive pool of information, unique in its scale in human history. There has never been anything like this Big Data before now about human mating habits!

Social scientists are eager to get their hands on this huge pool of information and study it for knowledge about human attraction and attachment. Raw data from dating sites is now being sold for studies to many universities including Yale, Stanford, the University of California, Rutgers, Princeton and Harvard, where professors and their teams are looking at how people reach out and choose partners in today's complicated world.

If you are interested in learning more about this, try a Google search with a phrase like "Dating study at Harvard." When I did that, the first item I found came from the Harvard Department of Sociology. You can do this search with any university and quickly get a sense of how important human mating habits are to researchers.

In the meantime, I enjoy being part of this enormous bank of knowledge. Plus, what the researchers are learning is just darned interesting. Google it for yourself and see if you agree!

For specific information about each dating site's Terms of Use or Privacy Policy be sure to read their fine print. You can always find the link to their (highly detailed) policies on the site's home page.

Do dating sites overstate their merits?

Sure. Word of mouth only attracts so many users. When advertisers get involved, you can expect that they'll sell the sizzle before they sell the steak. Their marketing departments need to make the dating sites sound wildly successful with lots of members, otherwise you won't join. Hundreds of millions of dollars are being spent every year selling dating sites to you—the consumer—promising you happiness and love. If they said that most users have a mediocre experience and are disappointed, no one would ever sign up.

What's realistic? You can check on how many members or unique visitors the dating sites get every month using business tracking services. Try looking at Online Personals Watch, which reports industry news on the dating industry. If you're really interested, you can sign up for their free and informative daily newsletter at www.onlinepersonalswatch.com.

You can also go to the business tracking service www.Experian.com and search their public articles and database for "Online Dating."

Online dating is such a big business now that statistics are often reported in the *Wall Street Journal, Fast Company, Fortune, Business Week* and *The New York Times*. It's not hard to learn that the industry is exploding with a growth rate of about 10% per year, in spite of the economic downturn. The advertisers are doing their job well.

Usually, the focus of fraud reporting is whether the users are lying about themselves or try to scam money off innocent victims, but there are some cases of dating sites padding their user lists by putting up false profiles. This is usually only a problem with new sites that are faced with the conundrum of needing to already have many members in order to attract many new members. If you stick with the larger, established sites, padded user lists shouldn't be a factor in your overall experience.

Getting involved with an online dating site is like any other consumer activity: Buyer beware! Don't assume that just because a dating site illustrates love and romance in their advertisements that this will be *your* result.

The dating site is a service and a tool for you to use to your best ability. It's up to you to you to use the tool actively. Just signing up and having a profile won't land you in one of those rosy-pictured advertisements. You need to diligently work the tool.

Making your choice of dating sites

If you are new to online dating, I would recommend starting with one of the large sites that covers the general population. If you feel comfortable with a monthly subscription and a three-month commitment, start on Match.com or EHarmony. If you'd like to keep your costs down while you're "learning the ropes", start on OKCupid. If you are over forty, I would not recommend starting with PlentyofFish just because so many of their users are younger.

After you have some experience, consider adding one of the niche sites if their theme appeals to you.

You should not sign up with more than one dating site to begin with. Here's why: most sites flag new people. "New" is exciting. "New" will get attention. Men who have been on the site for several months are eager to see new women. You will never get more attention that you get when you first put up your profile.

So, make your debut good. Put some work into your first profile.

And, allow yourself the time to learn what's going on and respond appropriately.

If you go up on more than one dating site at the same time, it will be hard for you to manage your experience thoughtfully. Take the online dating project ONE STEP AT

A TIME. Go up on one site. See how it goes for two or three months. Then, after you feel confident about how to respond to emails and set up dates, you can pull your profile down and go up on another. Or...stay up on two.

But NEVER put yourself up on more than two sites at a time. It's too confusing and you will find that there is some crossover anyway. You will see some of the same men on both. Just focus on one dating site first, then add another when you're comfortable. After a couple of months, you'll be eager to see who's "New", too!

Does it sound as though this is a long-term project? It may be. Did you think that you were going to meet the perfect man instantly? Possibly you could, but it's unlikely. You'd be better advised to mentally pace yourself for a longer project and, hopefully, be entertained and have a good time along the way.

The Top 17 Dating Sites for Women

Most of you know Experian as one of the major companies that tracks your personal credit score. They also track and score businesses and business trends. Since online dating now generates billions of dollars of revenue, it should not be a surprise that data about dating sites is tracked and analyzed. For more information about how their digital tracking works, go to www.experian.com/hitwise.

The top dating sites for women as ranked by Experian is listed in the chart below. The sites are ranked by numbers of hits each received, with data current as of this writing. By tracking the number of hits (live, real-time website views) a dating site receives, you will have real information about how active the site is.

Another way of ranking dating sites is by number of members, but this data is not always current. Plus, there are two problems in trying to rank sites by member totals. First, there is no way to sort out active from inactive members. Second, most paid sites allow people to sign up as members for free but they are not allowed to access to email unless they upgrade to a paid subscription. All free members are counted in the site's total, but this kind of mute member will not help your efforts to meet live and breathing men.

Often, these mute "members" are a high percentage of the total. For this reason, 100% free sites like OKCupid and PlentyofFish are more trustworthy because anyone you see on the site can communicate with you.

Note: Every effort was made to see that the following information was correct as of the time of publication but terms may have recently changed. Please check with each site for up-to-date information.

Dating Website	Fee or Free?	Fee information and description from their websites
www.PlentyofFish.com	Free	"POF has more dates, more relationships, more visits than any other online dating site."
www.Zoosk.com	Free	"Zoosk is the romantic social network that helps members create and share their romantic journeys."
www.Match.com	Free& Paid	Looking is free. Fee required to join and access all features and services. "We create romantic opportunities so singles are more likely to find someone special. Our mission is simple: to help singles find the kind of relationship they're looking for."

Dating Website	Fee or Free?	Fee information and description from their websites
ChristianMingle.com	Free & Paid	Membership is free. Fee required to become a subscriber to access all features and services. "ChristianMingle is an online community created specifically for Christian singles looking to meet other Christians."
DateHookup.com	Free	"DateHookup.com is a 100% free dating site...All we care about is you having a good experience using this site so you can tell your single friends to join!"
SeniorPeopleMeet.com	Free & Paid	Membership is free. Fee required for upgraded membership to use all features and services. "SeniorPeopleMeet.com is a community specially designed to cater to senior singles seeking mature dating."
www.SpeedDate.com	Free & Paid	Signup is free. Fee required for premium service to use all features and services. "Real dates in real-time."
www.OurTime.com	Free & Paid	Membership is free. Fee required to become a subscriber with access to all features and services. "A dating site that not only understands what it is to be over 50, but also celebrates this exciting chapter of our lives."

Dating Website	Fee or Free?	Fee information and description from their websites
www.OKCupid.com	Free	"We use math to get you dates. It's extremely accurate as long as (a) you're honest, and (b) you know what you want."
www.Badoo.com	Free & Paid	Free to sign up. Fee required to access expanded features. "Our mission: to provide the world's easiest, fastest and most fun way for people to meet each other locally and globally."
BlackPeopleMeet.com	Free & Paid	Membership is free. Fee required to become a subscriber with access to all features and services. "BlackPeopleMeet.com has built the largest community of African-American singles looking for love, relationships, friendship and dates."
www.Singlesnet.com	Free & Paid	Membership is free. Fee required to become a subscriber with access to all features and services. "Find your next first kiss today."
www.Yahoo.Match.com	Free & Paid	Match.com hosted on Yahoo.com. Membership is free. Fee required to become a subscriber to access all features and services.

Dating Website	Fee or Free?	Fee information and description from their websites
www.Mate1.com	Paid	Fee required to join and access all features and services. "Advanced search options, unlimited two-way chatting, free photo profiles and personalized voice greetings, Mate1.com continues to redefine the way singles meet, date and fall in love."
www.Eharmony.com	Paid	Fee required to join and access all features and services. "From single to soul mate."
www.Chemistry.com	Free & Paid	Membership is free. Fee required to become a subscriber with access to all features and services. "Chemistry is a premium offering from Match.com, designed especially for people who are looking for help in getting to know someone online so the first date feels like you're meeting for the second time."
www.Twoo.com	Free & Paid	Membership is free. Fee required for an unlimited account for full access to services. "Twoo is the most fun way to meet new people in your area."

Facebook Graph Search: Stay Alert for New Services!

A major player has entered the search market: in January, 2013, Facebook introduced Graph Search. As of this writing, it's too early to know how Graph Search will develop in the online dating market, but analysts think that one of Facebook's goals is to target online dating and the type of customers who use Match.com.

Facebook Graph Search will be free to use and has the potential to link a user's social media sites including Pinterest, Netflix, Yelp, Amazon and more. They could also offer Skype video chat, online chats and texting. Their technology has the power to set up private communication channels away from a user's normal Facebook pages, with the promise of keeping all dating activity private if desired.

Facebook has over a billion users and an enormous social graph that makes introductions through mutual friends possible in the future, if desired. Facebook, in fact, could be the largest social resource on the planet for singles who want to meet new people.

What could be completely disruptive for the paid dating sites like Match.com is that Facebook is 100% free to use. Their revenue comes from advertising. The paid online dating industry has been around for twenty-five years with only minor changes in their business model. Obviously, the tech giants at Facebook think that it's an industry ripe for disruption. Overall, the online dating market is growing year after year and seems to be recession-proof. When Facebook Graph Search matures and its tools are in place and working smoothly, singles might move to this full-spectrum dating service and away from the paid sites.

In the meantime, the strategy I suggested above is still a good one: Put your profile up on a free site (OKCupid) and, if you can afford it, one of the general population paid sites like Match.com or Eharmony.

And, don't forget: just because it's free doesn't mean you can afford to be careless about your profile. Do the work to make it as good as you can! The next chapter, *Step 3: Creating an Appealing Online Profile: Your Personal Brand,* has detailed instructions on what you need to do to present a stellar profile which will stand out from the crowd.

Read on!

STEP 3

CREATING AN APPEALING ONLINE PROFILE: YOUR PERSONAL BRAND

Your profile is your online dating personal brand and deserves your full attention. This chapter will cover all written elements in your profile from your user name to how you talk about your interests, sex, age and identity. It will also give you examples of good opening sentences that will grab the reader's attention and teach you how to write descriptions which avoid clichés. There are also tips on researching examples of effective profiles and a specific list of topics to leave out of your profile essays.

Preparing your online dating profile is like opening a local retail store. First, you need a store name that will advance and not sabotage your efforts. That's your user name. Then you need an appealing storefront to attract initial browsers. This would obviously be your collection of photographs. How to prepare good ones is worth a chapter by itself because photos are full of messages and non-verbal clues about your life-style. (See *Step 4: Preparing and Choosing Your Photographs.*) But that's only the beginning. You need worthwhile content inside to hold a visitor's attention.

The written content of your profile is where you are going to define yourself.

It is essential that your essays be expressive and well-written. If you are a thoughtful person hoping to attract a thoughtful man who is interested in creating a life with you, be prepared to put some time and effort into writing profile content that will appeal to your specific, prospective audience.

Dating sites and social scientists are busy mounting surveys on whether photographs or essays are the most important component in your profile. Research suggests that singles over forty are willing to look deeper and will read profiles thoroughly. Sure, there are plenty of stories about men who only look at pictures. We can all understand. Women do that, too. When I'm looking, if the man's picture is a turn-off, I don't bother reading what he has written. But, assuming that most pictures are neutral or good, within seconds I've gone on to read what the man has written.

This chapter is long and filled with examples and writing tips. It's not easy writing a compelling essay about yourself. Read the whole chapter and do the research I've suggested before your start. Trust that with you will be able to present yourself in words that are appealing and that inspire a man to want to get to know you better.

Let's start at the beginning of the profile with your user name.

CREATING A GOOD USER NAME

In the previous chapter, *Step 1: Getting Ready—Setting up an Email*, we discussed creating one user name for your dating site identity and using the same name for a dedicated dating email. Whether you chose to create an email for your dating project or not, your user name should do two things:

- Your user name should advance your identity in a positive way, or it should be neutral. Don't try to be too clever picking a name. A neutral name won't hurt you but a silly or inappropriate name can turn off lots of good prospects.

- Your user name should protect your true identity. Never use your real name.

With millions of people online already, don't be surprised if the user name you want is already taken. If your heart is set on using a certain name or phrase, here is a trick that always works:

- Add four or five numbers to the end of the word. Here's an example: The user name I wanted was "LifeisGood". I simply added four numbers to the end. There are thousands of combinations possible which meant that I was guaranteed to get the words I wanted.

Optimistic and pleasant phrases are a good choice. Here are some examples:

lifeisgood6789
candoitnow9876
inbloom4545
humorhappiness1234
happyhappy7890
birdsonwing3333
flowersong4321
musicharmony2222

Here are some types of phrases to avoid:

hottotrot4you
sexygirl4444
callmeanytime8675
loveschardonay4
cantwait67890
yourtoppick5678
milliondollarbaby4567

For some reason, men seem more prone to pick goofy or obnoxious user names. I've turned away from multiple profiles because the name was such a turn-off. "HotGuy4You", "LightYourFire3", "JungleRoar", "PackagetoUnwrap", "FastestCorvette", "NowChoseTheBest" were actual user names I ran across. Do they sound like chest-thumping to you, too? Thanks but no thanks.

HOW TO TALK ABOUT YOUR TRUE AGE

The easiest thing is to tell the truth. When you register with a dating site, they will ask you for your birth year. This calculates your age for your profile automatically. You can just leave it at that. If you are under fifty, that's a good choice. If you are under sixty, it's also the right thing to do. If you are just over sixty, however, I personally think that there could be some wiggle-room, providing that you tell the truth in your essay.

Searches for matches always include an age range. We tend to use Big Birthdays like forty, fifty or sixty as cut-offs. This means that a sixty-one year old will frequently be excluded in searches.

To avoid the cut-off at sixty, I rolled back my age three years by entering my birth year so my profile listed me as fifty-eight years old. I was actually sixty-one at the time. This gave me some ethical problems since I had never lied about my age ever before in my life. To clear things up right away, in my first essay on the site, I told the truth. The reason I gave for misrepresenting my age is that searches for matches include an age range and many men cut off their searches at sixty. My profile picture was current. In all the emails I exchanged with men, only one got huffy about this. Every other man appreciated my motives and the fact that I wasted no time revealing the truth. My choice to fudge my true age was not a deal-breaker.

You should examine your conscience and do what makes you feel comfortable. I am in no way suggesting that you permanently lie about your age. Nor am I suggesting that you go ahead and a meet a man under false pretenses. It is always easier to be completely truthful. Misrepresenting my age, however briefly, weighed on my conscience. Turning sixty hit me like a ton of bricks, and this is one of the ways I tried to deal with it. Hopefully, you will have an easier time, but if you are struggling with a Big Birthday, maybe my story can help you.

This illustrates that while many people will alter their statistics online to appear more appealing in searches, the extent of the lies is small. That does not excuse lying. However, it's true that many women take off a few pounds when listing their weight, many men add an inch or two to their height, and a few older people fudge their ages. Just make sure your photo is current and you "come clean" as soon as possible.

WHICH DISTANCE WILL WORK FOR YOUR SEARCH?

Dating sites build in a few basic statistics to your profile including height, weight, age and the range of miles in which you'd like to search for a date. For many people, the choice will depend on where you live. In Manhattan, a twenty-five mile range would be excessive but in Los Angeles, land of suburbs and freeways, it might be reasonable.

You should think about how much time you have available to "commute" to a date and how much you object to traveling. Some people don't mind. Others are working long hours or have family obligations and need a date close to home or work.

I recommend starting with a range of twenty-five miles if you live where driving is common. You can always change it later.

I live in the San Francisco Bay Area. There is a lot of terrain here—water and mountains—and many traffic bottlenecks that can make driving even a few miles a fist-clenching journey. I've been rejected by men in Marin County (twenty-five miles away) and men in Silicon Valley (fifty miles away) and even men in San Francisco (fifteen miles away) because they thought I lived too far away. And then there are other guys who don't measure distance. At the moment, I am seeing a man who lives in the South Bay in the hills above Silicon Valley. It's a one-hour drive from my front door to his house. I met him on OKCupid. Sure, I'd like it a whole lot better if he lived around the corner, but *c'est la vie*. He commutes to work daily and hates adding the extra distance. I don't mind driving, so usually I go to him.

My cousin met a woman on JDate who lived two blocks from his home. What incredibly good luck for both of them, since neither one wanted to commute! They have since sold both of their original houses and bought a lovely home together in the same neighborhood.

However it works out, distance is rarely a problem if you're in love.

PREPARING TO WRITE YOUR PROFILE ESSAYS

If you've already created a profile on LinkedIn, a timeline on Facebook and a homepage on Pinterest, you are already familiar with the basic experience of a curated presentation about yourself online. For an online dating profile, you are selecting from your interests, activities and personal history to create a short narrative that will be appealing to a stranger and spark his interest to learn more about you.

If you have no online experience, think about the selection process that goes into creating a resume for a job application. It's all about selection—what you choose to include. As you will see, what you leave out is just as important as what you put in.

It's easy to feel pressured about writing a good profile. Most of us can mentally picture men zipping through profiles, looking just at pictures and maybe skimming an essay. When the first few sentences sound the same, click after click, it's easy to imagine why some men pay more attention to the picture. Your goal, then, is to have a great picture and a terrific essay that will grab his attention in the first few sentences.

Before we get into the specifics about writing your essays, here are two tips to know about writing in general:

Writing Tip #1: Write your drafts in Microsoft Word, not directly on the site

If you write your essays in a word processing program like Microsoft Word, you can write as many essays as you wish. You'll also have the luxury of having friends review them before making them public. Do not write your initial drafts directly onto the site. Start a file for Online Profiles and save your essays. At the very least, save your drafts, then wait a day or two to review them. When you re-read them, are they dynamic and appealing? If not, edit, edit, edit.

You can easily copy and paste anything into the dating site. And...don't forget to check spelling—super easy—if you pre-write your essays in Microsoft Word. Avoid embarrassing spelling errors! Make Spellcheck your best friend.

Writing Tip#2: Do your market research before you start writing

No marketing professional would dream of launching a product without researching what is already on the market. Unless you have a working knowledge of the other profiles available to men, how can you know how to differentiate yourself and write one that will stand out from the crowd?

Use Google to research examples of good and bad profiles. Google is golden. Take a look at examples of profiles by going to Google and searching for "Good profiles for online dating." You can try other search phrases, but this one worked best for me.

Your search will turn up hundreds of examples, coaching websites and tips. Make notes on what you read. Like that first sentence? Jot it down. As you read, notice what catches your attention and what seems ordinary. There is more content in a Google search than could possibly be contained in any book. Plan to spend at least an hour researching what Google has to offer. Any time you're stuck, a good way to get your writing juices flowing is to go for a Google search. You will be full of new ideas and inspired to get back to work.

Don't be shy about reading what other women have published online. You should see what men see online to really learn and understand their experience. The easiest way to do this is to go to a dating site where you can browse for free and search the women's profiles. This may seem like "cheating" but it's really just market research.

Yes, this feels uncomfortable. But market research is essential if you are going to assemble an effective profile that will be noticed by your target audience. As much as I hate to fall back on the cliché "everybody does it," this is true, at least among my girlfriends. Smart, practical women want to know who else is at the party.

Put yourself in a man's position by trying to duplicate his experience of searching through hundreds of profiles. What will catch his attention? Does a lot of writing seem more appealing than an essay that includes bullet points and white space? Do you admire any opening sentences or turns of phrases? You can adapt anything you like to your own profile.

If you're stuck worrying about how to put your essay together, read, read and read more examples. You will soon see how it's done. Then, resolve to do better. Avoid what you see as clichés and commonplace adjectives.

While you're doing this research about essays, also pay attention to the photos. You'll want that photo information soon when you are creating your photo collection. For now, while you're browsing through other profiles for research, you want to notice which photos are dull and ineffective. Later, you'll know which poses to avoid.

Just a quick word about being competitive: I hate competing with other women. It should be obvious by now that I'm committed to the well-being and success of all women. And...it's simply the truth that in order to capture a man's attention online you need to put up a better profile than most other women, which might limit their chances. Ouch!

The way to do this as graciously as possible is to never compare yourself with other women. Do not practice negative advertising! Shine on your own merits! You never need to put anyone else down. Stay positive. Always.

THE FOUR KEYS TO WRITING GOOD PROFILE ESSAYS

Writing a profile essay is very similar to writing marketing materials, and it even has similarities to writing the copy on product packaging. Basically, you have only a few seconds to catch the attention of your target audience, then a few more seconds to please the reader so he's interested in learning more about you. Think about your essay as the product packaging a shopper sees walking through a store. Your photo is the color and shape. The content of your essay is the description on the box.

The main reason some women have disappointing experiences with online dating is because they have not set their profiles up for successful attraction and then, once the profile is "done", they don't work at promoting it by contacting potential dates.

Launching yourself online is a marketing project. You are building your personal brand.

Writing good profile essays will take some time, thought and effort. You may be a naturally gifted writer, or you may be someone who struggles with a blank page, but don't worry. Do your research as outlined above and follow the guidelines listed below and you will be able to write compelling essays about yourself.

All writers know that it's not easy writing about yourself. If you feel awkward and uncomfortable, be forgiving. The most important thing to remember is that you are trying to improve your life by taking on this project. And, you *will* improve your life. Be proud of the fact that you are trying your best. Stay truthful, follow the guidelines below and your sincerity and pleasure in your effort will shine through.

Here are the four keys to writing good profile essays. In the following pages, each key will be reviewed in detail with many writing samples you can use.

KEY #1: KNOWING YOUR TARGET AUDIENCE

Hold the image of the man you want to meet and pretend you are speaking just to him. Your writing should describe yourself in a way that will appeal to the man you wish to attract.

You are telling a story about yourself. It is not a work resume. It is not a factual bio. Of course, what you write should be truthful, but, most of all, it should tell your story, tailored to the ears of the man you want to meet.

It might help to write a quick description of that man. What would he do in his typical week? What is his career training? Is he analytical? Is he more of a poet? Do you want him to be sarcastic and politically active or more of a gentle, compassionate supporter of all points of view. Is he decisive? Does he love the outdoors? Is he committed to fitness and your vision of healthy living?

Jot down some quick notes about him and prop that page in front of you while you are working on your essay drafts. Take a deep breath. Relax. Think about the tone you would use in day-to-day speech to that man. You don't need to force anything. Just write as the person you truly are, speaking to the person you truly want to be with.

You cannot write an essay that will appeal to ALL men and you shouldn't want to do that. Forget universal appeal. Some of your statements will be turn-offs to some men, but that's fine. (See below for examples of statements that attract targeted men but turn-off others.) You don't want a random selection of men to respond. You want to pre-select who responds to you by TARGETING YOUR ESSAY.

KEY #2: KNOWING WHAT TO INCLUDE IN YOUR ESSAYS

Your essay should include specific examples of what you are doing or would like to do. Give examples. Avoid being vague. Choose only the most vivid adjectives and verbs. Remember, you are a storyteller. Don't be bland or write in generalities. Be specific! By describing specific examples of activities you genuinely enjoy, you create opportunities for a prospective date to resonate with your choices and imagine himself doing these activities with you.

Here are some examples of what to include as the vivid descriptions of your interests:

- If you want a creative, inventive man interested in good food, briefly describe your vision: *"I hope to cook our way through the cuisines of the world, together with you, savoring every bite."*

- If you want an adventurous man, describe one of your recent, favorite adventures: *"I love exploring the mountains and recently hiked trails in the Grand Tetons."* Avoid boasting if you've been hot air ballooning over the Serengeti! Instead, you can say *"see the pictures in my gallery"* which show you in adventurous poses. Be sure to caption the pictures with specific locations.

- Maybe you're an expert in harvesting wild mushrooms or want to spend your winter weekends skiing black diamond runs. Invite him to join you. Be sure to include a question: *"Is this what you'd like to do, too?"* Or, add an invitation: *"Exploring the underwater world is my favorite vacation. I can snorkel anywhere but dream of scuba diving the Great Barrier Reef. Could you join me?"*

- Maybe a more quiet pace suits you. Always be truthful. If you like sitting in comfortable chair reading a good book, say so: *"Nothing is more comforting than a quiet evening at home with my current favorite author. Even in the digital age, I love books. Sitting by a fire and reading beautiful sentences is a timeless joy."*

- If you want to be with someone athletic, write briefly about a sport you enjoy: *"A tennis game on Saturday morning is the perfect way to start the weekend, but I could play every day if I had the time."*

- If you like music and live concerts, talk about going out to the symphony, jazz or blues or rock concert: *"Yo-yo Ma played Beethoven at the symphony recently. I go to concerts when I can but at home I frequently listen to great concertos."* Or *"I sing in a choir and enjoy listening to vocal music."* Or *"Nothing beats a saxophone solo and a glass of champagne."* Or *"I play guitar, and can sing a wide repertoire of blue grass classics which will lift your spirits. You don't need to play claw-hammer banjo to be with me. Just tap your foot and smile!"*

- If you love art, don't be vague. Mention museums you've visited recently or an artist whose work impresses you: *"Like most people, I love the Impressionists, but it's Monet's garden scenes which really draw me in."* Or *"I can't go to museums and just look the paintings. Sculpture and craft works really call to me. Pottery, metal and glass are the materials I most love. Sometimes I wish I had become a potter, instead of a _____, because I love working with my hands. I do love my career, and also appreciate the desire to create or collect fine arts and crafts."*

- If you are talking a class, say so: *"I am studying _____ because it leads to a greater understanding of _____* *which is important to me because _____." Or "Tuesday evenings I'm studying Spanish so I can have a richer experience traveling in South America." Or "Mastering watercolors is a life-long quest. I paint landscapes and still lifes, and try to study weekly with a painting group."*

- If you are serious about healthy lifestyle practices, be sure to include a reference to your passion: *"Yoga and meditating are serious practices for me. Every day I find an hour to nurture myself, sometimes at a class, sometimes at home."* Or *"I'm a dedicated vegetarian. You should be comfortable with my choices."* Or *"Paying attention to healthy eating is a life-long passion. I care about nutrition and whole foods. No fast foods for me!"*

- If you love to host dinner parties and entertain, mention this: *"Inviting friends over for a good meal is not just a holiday event at my home. I love the laughter and warmth that comes from sharing good food and good friendship and know how to make my guests comfortable at my table."*

Are you a parent? Are your children younger or older?

Are you a parent of young children? Be careful here. You want to protect your children AND express your love for being with them. *"Going to the park with my son is my favorite spontaneous outing. The zoo is a special treat to do with special friends we both trust. Above everything, I hope to meet a trustworthy man."*

Are your children older? Trust is still important but their activity range is probably larger. Try saying something like this: *"I am still in the years when the school schedule of my children defines my months. Summers are more free. During the school year, I have deep responsibilities. It's a balancing act—my desire to have a social life and the need to see that my children's schedule is kept. If you're a parent, you understand."*

Note that some men who are not parents WON'T understand and will resent that your attention isn't freely available for them. OK. Just forget them. You need a responsible grown-up.

A word about sex and sexual desires

It's still a restrictive world out there about women publicly stating that they want sex. Most of the women I know believe that you can't talk about your sexual desires in "polite company." They would be excruciatingly uncomfortable writing about wanting sex in a dating profile. Of course, there is some wisdom in this if you are looking for a long-term commitment, since writing about wanting sex will most likely only attract men who are looking for one-night stands.

The audience for this book is women over forty who are looking for long-term romantic relationships, but social conventions make it hard for women to describe sexual desires as part of a traditional dating site profile.

Here's how you can discretely describe sex in your profile:

- Use the word "physical" instead of "sex" or "sexual".

- Illustrate a sensual moment. Here are five examples:

"For dessert, I can make a creamy tiramisu but surely you can think of other sweet endings to our perfect meal."

"I can cook a dinner party for eight, breakfast for two and thrill you in between."

"I love the feel of a man's chest. Watching him get dressed and buttoning his shirt is one of the gestures of love and intimacy I hope to share with the man in my future."

"Are you shy about skinny dipping? Me, too, unless I feel safe in your arms."

"Are you a morning person? I prefer long, sensual evenings when the alarm clock won't interrupt us and it seems we have all the time in the world."

And a word about humor

Well, of course you want to write a profile that will make your prospective date smile. But avoid saying that you have a great sense of humor. Everyone always has a great sense of humor! At least online. It's a better choice to say something self-deprecating or employ a few well-placed exclamation marks to keep the essay light.

Here are some examples of humor in profiles:

- Illustrate a small-scale, humorous failure: *"Snowshoeing looked so easy, but there I was flat on my face, panting."* Or: *"I don't embarrass easily but being at my high school reunion then finding a piece of salad stuck in my front teeth at the end of the evening made me cringe. Always check your teeth for spinach. I promise to tell you if you tell me!"*

- Describe what makes you laugh. Here are four examples:

  "Slapstick makes me howl with laughter. I'd like to say that rapier wit captures me but as embarrassing as this is to admit, physical comedy is my favorite."

  "I love to keep one of those daily calendars with either the Darwin Awards or other real-life jokes on my bathroom counter. That way, no matter what the day holds, I've started out with a laugh."

  "Do you like to read out loud? I love humorists and social commentators like Nora Ephron and David Sedaris—so much fun to read aloud with friends."

  "Every once in a while I love to ride a good roller-coaster, then laugh at myself for being so scared on the way down."

Don't dwell on trying to be funny. Avoid canned jokes. Your aim should be to evoke a smile of recognition, not a burst of guffaws. And if you feel uncomfortable trying to illustrate how witty you are, you are not alone. One or two examples of something humorous is more than enough.

Don't forget your photographs! You can include a picture of yourself in a humorous pose or in a funny setting. You have several opportunities to illustrate your bonhomie. Just be careful that in doing so you don't try too hard or you will only succeed in illustrating your stress. Relax and enjoy what you're writing. Your comfort and ease will come through.

KEY #3: KNOWING WHAT TO LEAVE OUT OF YOUR ESSAYS

If you have done your research and looked at examples of good and bad essays, you have a good idea by now of how boring a bad essay can be and how much of a turn-off poor spelling and bad grammar are. This makes the list of what to leave out of your essays pretty straightforward.

Here's what should NEVER be in your essays:

- Misspelled words. This is a great reason to write your drafts in Microsoft Word and use spellcheck.

- Lousy punctuation. When in doubt, use shorter, less complex sentences. You will never be faulted for writing in a direct style. This is another great reason to write your drafts in Microsoft Word, which will review your writing for basic grammatical errors.

- Obscure references. Don't try to prove how smart you are by mentioning a person or place that few have heard of. You'll have plenty of opportunities to prove the breadth of your knowledge on a first date.

- Overused suggested activities. Don't say that you love to walk on the beach. *Everybody* loves to walk on the beach. Pick something equally visual but more unique to you. Example: *"I love hummingbirds and enjoy spring gardens where I can watch them fly from flower to flower."*

It's VERY IMPORTANT to avoid describing these situations:

- Your horrendous divorce. So sorry that this happened to you, but going online is the time for you to focus on a new beginning. Do not discuss your divorce or breakups.

- Your anger at your job, your boss or your former in-laws. Sorry, again, but who wants to be with an angry woman? Leave your frustrations and irritation out of your essays.

- Your disappointments with first dates. OK, you haven't met a wonderful guy—that's why you are still online. Leave out your frustrations with the process and focus on improving your future!

- Any background on why you are single or any self-descriptions on why you think that it's difficult for you to pair up happily with a man. Save these revelations for your therapist or best friends! Don't shoot yourself in the foot by discussing any negatives of your past behavior.

Try to avoid these clichés:

- Dull and overused adjectives. Avoid *"attractive" "smart" "pretty" "warm" "funny" "kind" "honest"*. Instead, illustrate your point with an example.

- Instead of saying that you look good, say that you're *"Comfortable in a bikini."* If you want to make the point that you're well-read and keep up with current events, say that you *"Read The Economist magazine cover to cover."* If you're kind and love animals, say that *"you love rubbing a dog's tummy and feeding the birds".* If you're relaxed with your body say that you *"Enjoy summer so I can wear sandals and feel the breeze on my legs."* Remember that you don't need to comment directly on your appearance. Let your pictures speak for themselves.

- *"I love to travel."* Instead, try: *"My passport is always ready for a new stamp."*

Don't mention celebrities or fantasies:

- Save your fantasy life for pillow talk when you know someone much better. In your essays, stay grounded in real life if you want to attract a solid, grounded man. Flights of imagination are great for later. For now, in these short, introductory essays, stick to the here and now.

- Celebrity culture is a turn-off for many thoughtful adults. Avoid bringing the stars into your essays unless you want to sound like someone who doesn't have a life of her own.

Don't brag about what you have, where you've been or how successful your family is, or what good taste you have:

Nobody likes a spoiled kid and we like spoiled adults even less.

If you're affluent, it will show in your range of activities. If you went to Ivy-league schools and only want to date other Ivy grads, sign up for The Right Stuff which is an all-Ivy dating site. Maybe you were born into a family with many assets or maybe you worked very hard to build a comfortable lifestyle on your own. However you came by your rewards, don't boast about cars, houses, vacations or other signs of success. You can reference your hard work and entrepreneurial spirit but stay away from crowing about the payoffs.

KEY #4: KNOWING HOW TO WRITE THE FIRST THREE SENTENCES

In journalism, the first sentences are called "the lead." In comedy writing, they're called "the hook." In dating profiles, the importance of having a strong lead or hook cannot be overstated.

How much time do you have to catch a man's attention? Let's be realistic; you have only a few seconds if he is just browsing. Let's assume he likes your picture and looks down the page to your first essay. You have a few seconds to expand on the impression your picture has made, and, hopefully, persuade him to read further.

Depressing but true…it's not your fault. We are all used to going into stores and seeing hundreds of products flash by our eyes as we walk down the aisle. If we Google a topic, tens of thousands of results are available. There is just SO MUCH available information. We've become so used to tuning it out. Everyone is an editor now, skimming only the first lines for a nugget—something to sell us on the idea of spending more time without clicking through.

Read as many examples of profile essays as you can and notice which ones have strong openings. Why? What grabbed your attention? Take notes. You can re-write a strong first sentence to adapt it for your essay. Starting with a sentence that offers an adventure is always a strong lead.

Here are five examples of compelling first sentences:

- *"Diving with sharks was as scary as I thought it would be."*

- *"I drove from Paris to Berlin then onto Prague on my last vacation, stopping to enjoy the local cheese and soaking in historical landmarks along the way."*

- *"Self-publishing my first book has been a journey of discovery."*

- *"The view from Kilimanjaro is still on my wish list, but I'm ready to go!"*

- *"Being involved helping to build a strong, local community is my duty as a good citizen and I volunteer on a number of boards."*

If your essay starts with a strong action, a like-minded man will want to read more. If a guy doesn't admire what you're doing (and that's a risk if you mention anything political), no worries. You wouldn't want to date him, anyway.

Here are ten examples of strong, three sentence leads:

- *"On summer weekends you can find me hiking a local trail with binoculars for bird watching and having a picnic lunch. Watching eagles or hummingbirds fills me with wonder for* the natural world and an insatiable curiosity to explore and learn more. Recently, I became a certified scuba diver, fulfilling a life-long dream to go for underwater adventures."

- "The piano in my apartment is often a hub of activity for friends singing Broadway classics after a delicious potluck dinner. I love arranging good times for friends that center on food, music or enjoying an evening out at a show. Watching out for the positive enjoyment of those around me feels natural."

- "Starting a business this year has been the adventure of a lifetime, between designing and launching a product, training staff and keeping the back-office organized. I thought that my MBA would prepare me but I am humbled by how much there is to learn doing hands-on entrepreneurial work. I'm eight months into my new company with a greater appreciation for hard work and commitment to a vision."

- "That trip through Tuscany is still at the top of my wish list. Learning to cook Italian food in an authentic Italian kitchen is how I would like to spend my next vacation. Good wines with my hand-made pasta, then maybe a bicycle ride in the countryside or hiking Cinque Terra on the coast would round out the trip. And, as an art lover, I'd have to visit Florence and be dazzled with every view."

- "Homegrown tomatoes with fresh basil from my herb garden make the best summer salads. On warm nights you can find me in my garden, enjoying the sweet night air then relaxing with a cup of tea on the back porch. Gardens and parks are my sanctuaries, my oasis from the hustle and busy hours of everyday life."

- "Can you walk into a room of strangers and start confidently 'working the room?' It makes me nervous, too, but it's a skill I've had to master in my career, and now, I really enjoy meeting new people from all walks of life. My favorite stories are those from families who have moved to the US and had *to reinvent themselves. I admire their resilience and courage since my own family did that, three generations ago."*

- *""Stroke hard, hard, now!" The rapids crashed around us as everyone on board the raft pulled on their oars as hard and fast as we could. "Class III..??" I thought, loving the adventure but also scared out of my mind. I'd taken up white water rafting to have outdoor adventures with built-in company."*

- *"I spent two weeks volunteering for Habitat for Humanity, helping to build new homes on Native American reservations. The crew came from all over the country and many of them volunteered every year. It was the most fulfilling vacation I could imagine."*

- *"Studying Spanish in an immersion program was something I'd always wanted to do and last summer I had the chance to stay in San Miguel Allende. The daytime was filled with classes but nights found me exploring this lovely colonial city where vibrant colors and the sounds of musicians are everywhere. I can't wait to practice my newfound language skills exploring Central and South America, hopefully with a new love."*

- *"Catching the home run baseball at Dodger Stadium last summer should happen to every lucky person! I was on cloud nine—even the hot dogs tasted like the greatest food ever made. The ball now sits on my desk, a reminder that sometimes you can be at the right place at the right time. Maybe, since you're reading my profile, it's the right place for you, too!"*

BEING SMART ABOUT PROTECTING YOUR IDENTITY

You're prudent and probably more than a little bit nervous about writing something in your essay that will reveal your true identity. Well, it's not always a simple matter to include specifics about your activities and interests while also scrubbing the essays of any clues that could lead to knowing where to find you.

Here are the obvious things to avoid:

- Don't use your real name for any part of your user name.
- Don't include your phone number, email or specifics about your neighborhood in your essays.
- Don't identify your workplace, school or church.
- If you're in a dorm, say nothing about your living arrangements.
- If you live alone, say nothing about your living arrangements.
- If you have an unusual dog, don't identity the breed.
- If you regularly go to a coffee shop or bar, don't give the name or neighborhood.
- If you work out at a gym, don't identify which one.
- If you're taking a class, don't say where or what time.
- If you have a favorite hiking or running trail, don't name it or identify the park.
- If you have kids, don't describe them. Consider not including pictures of them in your gallery.

Protecting your anonymity is wise until you feel safe revealing your identity to a man AFTER you have researched him and can reasonably feel that he is trustworthy. See *Step 8: Identity: Tips for Learning His True Identity and When Should You Reveal Yours.*

If you make sure that your presence online cannot be traced back to you in real life, there is no reason why you shouldn't relax and enjoy yourself with the online experience. "Shopping" for men online is fun. Reading other people's profiles is pure entertainment. It's touching, painful, funny, inspiring and better than fiction.

Be smart about joining the party and have a good time while you're there.

STEP 4

PREPARING AND CHOOSING
YOUR PHOTOGRAPHS

Do you feel pressured and worried about which photographs to include in your profile? Maybe you don't feel confident that your photographs make you look attractive. Maybe you're just not sure what to do. You are not alone!

All of my girlfriends have felt the same way, and I did, too! No one here is a professional model. We worried about whether our photos made us look heavy or made us look old. We didn't know what's best: indoors, outdoors, which clothes to wear, alone or with other people, doing something or just standing there. And we wondered whether we should include a picture of our favorite cat or dog.

Anyone who has done research on how to create a good online profile has run across claims and studies saying that men are more influenced by pictures than profile essays. This just adds to our pressure! Serious academic research has been done tracking men's eye movements across photos of women. What are they looking at? Eyes? Breasts? Smiles? The cat...?

The answer is "all of the above."

That's not very helpful, of course. What is more helpful is actual research on which types of profile photographs received the most responses from men and whether those responses actually converted to a genuine email contact. Remember: the goal of your profile is to attract men with whom you can first have email contact and then convert that contact into meeting in person if you so choose.

It all starts by being realistic about what kinds of photographs will attract the kind of men you'd like to meet.

LEARN WHICH ARE THE MOST EFFECTIVE PHOTOS

OKCupid has a large database of the responses to profile photos. In 2010 the site published results of a 7,000 photo survey analyzing which poses got the most responses. You can find the survey by going to Google and searching for *OKCupid: The 4 Big Myths of Profile Pictures.*

What they learned shook up some entrenched beliefs about which photos are best for your profile. For example, the conventional wisdom is that your primary photo should show your face. OKCupid learned that a photo showing an interesting activity that catches the viewer's attention also receives a lot of responses, *even if your face can't be seen!*

Amazing. It's obvious that you must include a photograph that features your face somewhere in your profile, but it's not mandatory that it be your primary picture, according to this survey's results. Let's salute those women who are courageous and are willing to try something bold and original! I always used a close-up of my face as my primary profile photograph but the OKCupid survey shows that there are other creative choices.

There have been many studies about eye contact with the camera. OKCupid's research shows that both eye contact and smiling is good. Eye contact without a smile or without what they call a "flirty face" is not effective. So, look at the camera and smile!

The suggestions I'm going to make for your profile photographs combine results from my own personal experience, the experience of my friends, and a synthesis of research and survey results that I've read and studied about online dating site results. I've tried to sort through all of this to come up with practical suggestions for you to take the worry out of creating and choosing your profile pictures.

Photography is an art and selecting good photographs can take a trained eye. Let's get started by understanding that each photograph tells a message. Your online messages should all coordinate and support your goals.

YOUR PHOTOS SHOULD SUPPORT YOUR GOALS

Photographs reveal information about your personality, values, beliefs, habits and goals in direct and subtle ways. Even the background behind you, which you might not notice, tells stories to the observer. I have friends who use pictures taken in their home or garden, and were concentrating so hard on how they look in the picture that it never occurred to them to look at what was happening behind them.

It is very important that you pay attention to all elements of your photographs: the subject (you), the background (if it's not a super-tight close-up) and anything you are wearing or doing which could carry a message.

If you are presenting yourself as a person with many interests, chose photographs that show you involved in an activity. My friend, Amanda, is a wonderfully smart, talented woman who does many things very well but for her profile pictures, she only chose head shots. About fifteen of them. All basically the same pose. With her doing nothing but sitting there. The net result was a message of repetition and self-absorption. Instead, Amanda could have chosen photos of herself painting, hiking, playing piano or singing and delivered the message that, indeed, she is active and interesting.

If you want to be treated with respect as a woman interested in a long-term relationship, don't post pictures that make you look like a casual party girl. Another friend, Sue, is a successful corporate manager. For some crazy reason, she chose pictures of herself in skimpy tee-shirts, showing cleavage and drinking beer. She thought it would make her appealing to more men. Maybe she was right about the numbers, but Sue complained to me that the only men who contacted her wanted quick, sexual dates and nothing else.

Your photographs should illustrate the life you lead. Or, if you'd like to reinvent yourself, they can illustrate the life you want to lead.

This is why it's important to understand what you hope to accomplish by putting up a dating profile. Men will respond to the image you project. My friend, Sue, looked sexy and drunk in her pictures, so it's no surprise that she didn't attract men who were interested in having conversations with her.

Keep Your Photos Truthful and Timely

Using current photos is always the best policy. Nobody wants to feel tricked and if you misrepresent your appearance by using a ten year old photo, it will only backfire on you when you meet the man.

If you're not happy with your appearance, that could be motivation for self-improvement. A new hairdo or new eyeglass frames are examples of affordable changes that can make a big difference to your self-esteem.

THE FIVE BEST TYPES OF PHOTOS TO INCLUDE

My recommendation is that you include between three and five well-chosen photographs in your profile. Even if the dating site allows you to upload more, resist the temptation. This is not the place to create a full photographic essay about your life and interests. You can do that on Facebook or Pinterest.

What you want to do here is create an interest in getting to know you better. It only takes a few photographs to accomplish that. When you include more, you also increase your risk of including something unappealing. Why create an additional risk?

What you want to do is attract a man so you can have contact with him and move towards meeting in person. Your photographs have one vital but simple task: to initiate interest. Hopefully, your viewer will go on to read your essays in which your personality will shine.

The five best types of photos to include in your profile

Photo #1: Headshot: a flattering close-up of your face with your eyes looking directly into the camera. Smile. See below for suggestions on the best angle.

Photo #2: Full-body photograph: a photograph showing all of your body, standing or sitting, preferably showing you doing something that will start a conversation for an email exchange. Don't freeze up worrying about what activity to include. Just be sure to include at least one photograph that shows you from head to foot.

Photo #3: Travel photo: a photograph of you in a setting away from home. If you don't have the Eiffel Tower, a beach or beautiful tree will do just fine.

Photo #4: Activity-based photograph: a photograph of you involved in an activity you like. This can be from the waist-up or full-body. It should be simple for the viewer to identify the activity. You'll find suggestions for activity-based photographs below.

Photo #5: Animal photo: a photograph of you with your dog or cat. There are mixed reviews about this one but I think that if you love hiking with your dog or if your cat is very important to you, including one photograph of you with your pet is reasonable. Don't use this as your primary photo and make sure that you are the main subject, not the pet.

Taking the perfect headshot: What is the best angle for women over forty?

We can learn a lot from Hollywood photographers who knew where to position the camera. Holding the camera above your head so you are looking up is a very flattering angle.

You can do this most simply by holding your camera at arm's length above your head and smiling into the lens. Or, you can have a friend stand on a ladder. Your best results, of course, would be to use a professional photographer in a studio setting with good lighting. If you are willing to be patient and try different types of lighting plus have someone to help, you can get good results right at home.

Here is the headshot I used on my own profile:

This photo was cropped close to my face.

This is the original photograph, uncropped.

My son stood on a ladder to get above me and I looked over my shoulder. It was a great way to smooth out my neckline! My body was standing facing to the left side of the camera so I had to really turn my head. When you tilt your chin back, turn your head and look up, gravity does all the work for you! And, it's not such a big change from how you really look face-to-face. None of my dates ever commented or complained that my photo had misrepresented my appearance.

The photo I posted and the one that received the best response was the close-up of my face. At first, I did put the original, uncropped photo up on my profile and very quickly learned that my cleavage was attracting a lot of men and a few comments that made me feel uncomfortable. I resubmitted the photo by cropping out the cleavage and focusing on my face. I had no problems with inappropriate comments after that.

The activity-based portrait: Make it easy to start a conversation with you

Some photographs just invite comments or questions. Keep in mind that most men feel awkward sending you an email and will be looking at your profile for something to help them get started. You can make it easier to open a conversation by including photographs that show you doing something interesting. A close-up of your face may be beautiful, but the comments flowing from this are limited. Take pity on these poor guys and give them a boost by including a least one picture of you involved with an easily recognizable activity they can comment on.

There's no need to fake anything. What you do in your daily life should provide enough material. Maybe you have some photographs already, but, if not, here are some ideas:

- If you love gardening, include a picture of you working in the garden

- If you're a tennis or golf player, hold the racquet or club
- If you're a musician, include a picture with your instrument
- If you love birding, take a picture with your binoculars or next to a bird feeder
- If you love reading and books, a picture of you with a book would be great
- If you like to ski, pose on the slopes
- If you're an artist, hold an art brush in front of a canvas
- If you love cooking, smile for a picture in your kitchen
- If you love to travel, show yourself at an interesting destination
- If you enjoy hiking, pick your favorite panoramic trail
- If you're a writer, smile over your laptop or notepad

You can see that it's easy to create an activity-based photograph of yourself. It doesn't need to be a professional, spectacular portrait. It just needs to be interesting and worthy of a comment. If you wish to maximize your potential for quality responses, be sure to include at least one or two of these in your profile.

Here's the activity-based photograph that I included in my own profile:

The caption for this photo is "Favorite travel activity"

Scuba diving is not an activity that everyone does, but as it turns out, the wonderful man in my life whom I was lucky enough to meet online is also a diver. His response to my profile and eagerness to meet me was the direct result of this photograph! And...it doesn't even show my face!

Should you use a professional photographer?

You may have a library of appealing digital photographs of yourself, but if you don't, expect to invest some time and possibly money in creating them.

If you ask a friend to take pictures of you, follow the guidelines in this chapter on how to prepare and chose your poses. Your cost? Probably a cup of coffee or glass of wine.

If you go to a professional photographer (highly recommended) expect to pay from $100 to $200 for head-shots. Check your local photographers online for specials. Remember that real estate professionals all need head-shots. If you know anyone in real estate, ask them who does their office's portraits.

Match.com recommends a service that finds photographers in your area. Check out http://www.lookbetteronline.com/match/. This service is offering twelve dating photographs from a forty-five minute photoshoot for $149. It's possible that this low price is only for a promotion, but the service still sounds good if you can afford a professional photographer.

It's understandable that you might want to avoid spending money for your profile photographs when everyone has a decent camera these days, but don't skimp on the effort to picture yourself as attractive. It's worth the time and money investment, as your photo is the most powerful tool on your profile.

AVOID THESE TYPES OF PHOTOS

There are some photographs that you probably have available which should not be included in your profile. They are:

- Group photos: Help yourself stand out by not including a picture of yourself in a crowd. Your profile should focus on you.

- Photos that have clumsy cropping: Is that a hand on your shoulder? Either learn Photoshop to be able to edit random body parts out of your profile pictures, or avoid using photos that will create embarrassing questions.

- Photos of you drinking: Surveys consistently show that it's best to leave alcohol out of your photos.

- Old, outdating photos: We've covered this already. Don't use photos that are seriously out of date. If a man expects to meet a younger you, he will feel as though you have lied to him when he sees you in person, just as you would if he misrepresents his appearance. It's not a great start for a first date.

- Photographs of your children: No one should be included in your profile without their permission. For your younger children, there are obvious safety issues. For your older children, they may not want to be included in your dating efforts. Check with them first! I've seen many photos of men with their grown children and while I enjoyed seeing the families, I wondered how the daughters and sons felt about being included.

Cleavage and skin: How much to show?

If you're fit and over forty, showing off your body's contours is definitely one way to get more attention. The question is: what kind of attention? This is going to depend on how you are dressed and how you pose. If you're on a bicycle in a tight, spandex cycling outfit, your great shape will be just an obvious as posing in a low-cut dress.

Consider your goals and what kind of relationship you hope to have with a man you meet on the Internet. Do you envision that he'll be bringing you home to meet his parents? If so, dress conservatively and don't let your breasts hang out in your profile photos.

Summer dresses, shorts and swimsuits are all good. Just stay away from overtly flirty poses if you expect to be taken seriously as a candidate for a long-term relationship. Remember, your photographs should illustrate your values and goals.

STEP 5
HOW TO READ AND DECODE A MAN'S PROFILE

Every profile is full of clues about the personality, values, beliefs, habits and goals of the person who wrote the essays and chose the photographs. Because our goal in this book is for you to have a good time dating and be able to move towards creating a long-term, loving relationship in your life, your ability to decode a man's profile is an important skill in making positive, informed decisions about which men you would like to meet face-to-face.

Reading a profile with an analytic frame of mind is a lot like being a detective. You should be actively looking for clues. Most of the time, this will be easy. Red flags will jump out at you or things he says or demonstrates in the photos will resonate with you and you'll want to learn more.

No profile is completely neutral. Every profile you read will be like a tiny novel about his life. Who needs fiction?!! Online dating gives you access to hundreds of real-life stories, some appealing and some so repulsive they'll give you shivers. Just remember: amid the shouts and murmurs, there are decent men, in your area, who just want to meet a good woman. Maybe they wouldn't win a Pulitzer Prize for their profiles, but all they have to do is be honest and be interesting enough so that you want to take it to the next step, which is contacting them. (Yes, *you* will take the initiative and reach out. See the *Step 7: How to Initiate Contact with a Man Online*.)

Let's start with the photographs, since that's what will catch your eye first.

HOW TO INTERPRET A MAN'S PROFILE PICTURES

Profile photographs have a lot of information to offer you beyond the superficial impression. They can teach you about the man's values, beliefs, habits, goals, and quite a bit about his past history if you know how to look and evaluate each photo.

The key here is to not look passively. Once a man has caught your attention, put on your best observation radar and take a closer look at his clothing, anything he's holding, what's in the background and any companions or animals in the photo. There are often captions with each photograph that can reveal information

A photograph is never neutral. Whether it was taken by the man to show off his pecs—I hope not—those bathroom shots are for juveniles or insecure guys flaunting their bodies. Each profile photo is a gold mine of information for you.

Here are some questions you will need to ask yourself when you look at a man's profile photos. Taking notes is a good idea if you're really serious about contacting a man who catches your interest.

What if he doesn't have a profile picture?

This answer is super simple. Click delete and move on. Do not spend one second on the profile of a man who has not posted even one picture. Don't read the essays which often include some whining complaint about his older camera that won't upload. Just forget it. There are plenty of other fish...

yes, oh so many other men. You don't need to waste a moment with anyone who can't put up a picture.

Analyzing his photos

The man in the profile made a decision that he wanted to include the single or multiple photographs that you're looking at. If there is only one profile picture, it puts even more pressure on that one item to convey information. His decision to include this photo leads you to your first and most important question: "Why did he think that this is his most appealing picture?" If you can answer that question, you will go a long way towards understanding how the man wants to present himself to the world. You will then be able to think about whether that choice is appealing to you or not.

Let's look at several common styles of profile pictures:

Is his photo a head-shot only?

Possible message #1: He's not happy with his body and wants to feature his face only. Check his self-description of body-type. If indeed, he is listing "several extra pounds" you might be looking at a guy who is not fit and has body image issues. Possible message #2: He's a very smart, analytical type who understands how much information a photograph contains. He may be trying to control the flow of information.

Is his photo a cropped version of a larger group shot? Is there a hand on his shoulder?

Perhaps he thinks that this is a particularly flattering picture of his face and he's with someone whose identity he wants to protect, like his daughter. Or, there's a woman in the shot he's cropping out. The message: a cropped shot says that he doesn't care enough about the online dating process to put the effort into creating a good profile picture that features only him. These days, when everyone has a camera on his or her phone, it seems careless to me that a man won't make even a small effort to present himself in a flattering light. Frankly, I think you'd want to spend your time with someone who cares more about the process. Plus, there's always the chance that he has cropped out his wife.

Is he standing in front of a car or motorcycle?

Well, I guess he wants you to know that he can go fast, or he's making a statement that a vehicle is his prized possession. You may learn something from the make of the car—if it's a 1930 Duisenberg classic car, the guy has style! And money! If you are not comfortable riding on the back of a motorcycle, beware of the man who includes his bike in his main profile pic.

Is he standing at the helm of a boat?

Personally, I enjoy these because I like being on boats. Interestingly, of the dozen or so men who contacted me with boat pictures, only two actually owned sailboats. Still, you can get the message that he wants you to think about him as an outdoorsman.

Is he standing in a backyard or on a deck?

Take a look at the background. Is the yard small, suburban? Is the deck overlooking an expansive view? What does he say about being a home owner? If you're a gardener, you want to pay special attention here. Does the landscaping interest you? Can you see yourself in this setting?

Is he standing near a recognizable monument?

Nothing says "I've been to Paris" like a photo in front of the Eiffel Tower. Take a close look at his clothes and imagine yourself walking the Left Bank with him. If this is well within your comfort zone, congratulations! Go for it!

Are there other people in his photograph?

If his profile picture(s) includes other people, what do you think the relationships are? And why did he include them in his profile? If it's a happy crowd shot, maybe he wants you to know that he's extroverted and likes to socialize with groups of people, and hope that you will join him. If the other people are clearly family, especially his children, the message clearly is that he's letting you know immediately that he's a devoted family man and his top priority is his children.

Are all of his photos the same?

Be attentive if all of the photos a man has posted show the same angle or the same, tightly cropped head-shot. Possibly he thinks this is his most flattering photo or possibly he has something to conceal. You might make a mental note about this.

Men typically post fewer photos than women, and it's legitimately possible that he just doesn't have a lot of photos in a variety of poses. Still, if you see many photos with the same close-up, look for other clues that maybe he's not fit. Ideally, you'd like to see at least a facial close-up and a full-body shot. It's not a fatal flaw in a profile if you don't. Just be alert.

What else can you learn from the context of his photographs?

Backgrounds are immensely important. If he's standing in front of a most unflattering background (off-kilter wall pictures, for example) this says something about his situational awareness. You can often learn many clues about his living space by looking at what's behind him. If it's a photo taken at work, is he in a cubicle? If he's athletic, has he placed himself in a sporting background? Is he presenting a professional portrait, posed against a well-lit background, the whole composition designed to flatter and confirm his intelligence, competence and professional expertise?

Most important, what's your instant, overall reaction? Do you like what you see?

Men wearing skimpy clothing. Why do they do that?

Multiple websites have sprung up to laugh at men who photograph themselves in beef-cake poses. Personally, I'd rather see a guy, fully-dressed, holding his Pulitzer Prize, than some half-naked man with a would-be six-pack in front of his bathroom mirror. There is something infinitely sad about a middle-aged man needing to lead off the conversation with the size of his muscles. I do like firm muscles, but I'd rather that they are part of a whole package: brains, heart, sense of humor, good taste and curiosity about the world.

Sometimes you'll run across a man in a skimpy swimsuit. If he's a world-champion windsurfer, this is legitimate! If he's a lonely divorced guy in his hot tub, well, maybe those swinger movies from the 1970's are still interesting to you, too. In that case, go have fun.

What does his wardrobe say?

You can learn a lot from the clothes a man is wearing. A blazer, casual Friday, a tee shirt and too-tight jeans, a hoodie, sports fan memorabilia and hats: all have information for you about his taste, his grooming and how he wants you to think about him.

Remember, the man chose this picture as his best offering. If he's clearly disheveled, consider the possibility that the guy is self-destructive. Sabotaging himself in a profile picture may just be the tip of an unhappy iceberg.

I think the most important message is compatibility. Can you see introducing a man dressed like that to your friends? Would you want to walk down the street with him? Our culture is very casual these days, but beware of the man who can't put together his wardrobe for a profile picture. Casual is fine but a slob is still a slob.

It's hard to tell a man's income from his clothing in this, the age of the Silicon Valley billionaire hoodie tee shirt, jeans-wearing, running-shoe-every-day lack of dressing-up standards. Call me old-fashioned, but I like a man in a suit. Or, at least a blazer and a shirt that buttons. But, at the end of the day, what counts is if he's clean and neat. If you see food stains on his shirt (and—believe it or not I've seen this on profile pictures) hit delete!

True age and photographs

Just like older women, men are tempted to shave a few years off their age. This, of course, becomes very obvious if they use a ten year old photo and show up for a first date looking much older. Once, I had a first date with a man who was shockingly older. When I asked, he admitted to using a twenty-five year old picture which showed him with a lot more hair and a more trim waistline.

I should have paid attention to the details in his photo—like the eyeglass frames from the 1980's and the sideburns. Dead giveaways!

Generally, you won't have a big problem with this since repeated surveys show that most people shave less than five years off their true age. You probably won't be able to decode the truth from most profile pictures in which the clothing and grooming are reasonably current.

Nevertheless, it pays to be alert to any clues. Look for current style clothing, eyeglass frames and hairstyles. If you see wide lapels, shoulder pads, sideburns and mullets, run for the hills! Of course, you can't tell with bell bottom pants these days since they are making a (dreaded) comeback.

What does his body language say?

We all know something about body language by now. If the man is standing with his arms tightly crossed against his chest, he may be anxious and very shy. If he's smiling broadly with his arms open wide, this is a welcoming, extroverted guy. If his eyes are downcast, maybe he doesn't really want to be doing the online dating exercise. If he has a drink held up to his lips, watch out—there may be too much alcohol in his life since he thinks that this is an appealing pose.

Pay close attention to how you react to his body language. Are you drawn to be with him? Does his pose make you want to shy away?

If there are other people in the photo, what kind of posture does he have in relation to them? Is he relaxed? Is he directed the crowd? Does he look happy? Is there action depicted? Are they eating? Maybe family events that celebrate food are his favorites. Maybe he's a great cook. Check out the prose in his essays to see if there is any relationship between the photograph(s) and what he writes about.

How do his hands look?

Not all photos show hands, but when they do, you are in luck. Take a close look at his grooming. Are his nails trimmed? Can you imagine those hands touching your intimate places? If necessary, hit the zoom button so you can get a closer look at his hands in the picture. Is he wearing a ring? Can you see a tan line where a wedding ring might have been? Is he wearing a watch and do you have an opinion on the style?

Finally, think about the overall mood or feeling

Try to choose one or two adjectives that you would use to describe his photo(s). "Cheerful." "Obsessive." "Outgoing." "Thoughtful." Avoid over-used adjectives like "Attractive." Try to pick words that will describe his personality, based on the evidence he has provided. Remember, he wants you to interpret the photo(s) he has chosen for a positive outcome for him. Are you willing to agree?

Make your best choice

Think critically. There are lots of men online. Many will be an outright waste of time. You can maximize your results for positive experiences looking carefully and analytically at a man's profile pictures. Select the ones which seem most in sync with your own values. Discard profiles with pictures that are silly or just turn offs. For pictures that you rank "neutral," give the man the benefit of the doubt. Not everyone is photogenic, but everyone offers a lot of information that you can use to learn about personality, beliefs, values, habits and priorities in even the most casual photograph.

Good luck in your interpreting! Use the knowledge you have gained in decoding profile photographs to make informed decisions.

HOW TO READ AND DECODE A MAN'S PROFILE ESSAYS

No online presentation is a blank slate. From the choice of screen name through the final word of an essay, some guy sat in front of his computer thinking about what would be the best way to attract women. Just remember, the men are as nervous and self-conscious as you are. It's a strange and difficult process setting yourself up for online approval or disapproval. Some compassion is needed. BUT, that doesn't mean that you should waste your time. Click rapidly through the profiles that flunk your most rudimentary requirements.

Here's a suggested list of the ten basics you need to see in a man's essay:

- Correct spelling and good grammar
- Evidence that he's sincere about the process: you want to see that some effort went into creating his profile
- He is confident
- A generally positive attitude
- He should be ready for a fresh start: no negatives about past women
- Interesting activities
- An ability to avoid clichés

- No outlandish, obvious bragging
- Good manners
- Any threats to safety are an instant deal-breaker

Let's take a closer look at each of these and the specific red flags to look for in a man's profile.

Evidence of a basic, good education: Correct spelling and good grammar

Would you be comfortable with a man who is essentially illiterate? If you are college-educated and love to read, you'll have a hard time with a man who can't spell and who doesn't have the presence of mind to use Spellcheck. With all due respect for the many talented dyslectic men in the world who have achieved great things in spite of their struggle with words, any man online who can't write a properly spelled and punctuated paragraph is going to frustrate you. Click away quickly.

Is he sincere about the process? The length of his essays is a measure of effort

Take an overview of the length of his profile. Is it painfully short? A man who is serious about finding a partner will put some effort into creating an appealing presentation.

Skipped questions and super-short answers aren't a good sign that he is on a sincere search. Depending on how interested you are in other factors (ex: distance, the few bits of information he's offered) you may chose to ignore his lack of effort and contact him anyway. Some men just don't have faith in the opportunity to meet a good woman through an online dating site and feel that putting in a lot of effort is a waste of time. This is too bad. You could ignite his faith in the process by sending him a quick message. Your anonymity is protected so you have nothing to lose but 60 seconds of your time. Just don't expect much in return.

On the other hand, if a man has put NOTHING in his profile, click away.

Is he confident?

How many essays open up with a sentence like this: "I'm not much of a writer." Or "I'm not sure how to get started." Or "I've never tried this before so here goes..."

I wish those guys had some more confidence and presence of mind. To open up a presentation by hanging your head, scuffing your feet and hemming and hawing is so discouraging. These men should be aware that everyone is in the same position—feeling awkward and unsure of what to say—so we just go ahead and do our best without wallowing publicly in our insecurities. If he's that nervous writing an essay, imagine how nervous he's going to be when he meets you!

Since this book is written for women over forty, I'm assuming that you, the reader, are someone who has some experience in the world. You have already had some adventures. You want some more. You are probably starting to wonder about what lies in store for you in your remaining years on Earth, and you are committed to making those years the very best that you can. You want a partner who shares your sense of adventure and wants to make sure your years are full, enriched with love, learning and new experiences.

This takes courage. It takes bravery. You can't be endlessly afraid of doing something new. Keep your chin up and your spine strong. Do not scuff your feet before you take a new step.

I feel sorry for those men who need to tell you how scared, unsure and uncomfortable they are. Yes, I really do feel sorry for them. But, I don't want to spend any of my precious time with someone who is not excited about facing the future and brave about creating it. Stick with the guys who demonstrate that they know what they are doing or, at least, are brave enough to do something new without whining about it.

You need a general, positive attitude: The importance of tone in his writing

You can get a sense pretty quickly about whether a man is upbeat. Is he humorous? Do his sentences make you smile? Can you imagine enjoying the company of this guy at a party? Could you see him as the life of the party? It's not easy to convey this in the first profile essay, but a general sense about whether the man is an optimist should be something you are looking for.

Don't worry too much about humor. It's hard to be witty and write comedy. If his essays can make you smile, that's terrific and an added appeal. But basically, you just want to get a sense that this is someone who laughs easily, smiles readily and enjoys life.

You should also be alert for signs that he is genuinely looking forward to meeting an interesting woman. Look for positive statements like "I'm happy when a woman is open and creative." Or "I enjoy exploring new places with someone I love." Or "When a woman says what she truly thinks, I'm pleased."

You want to spend time with a man who clearly enjoys the company of women.

Is he ready for a new start? Beware of negative examples

Profiles often include negatives that reflect a man's past experiences. Usually, this is a very bad sign. You don't want previous girlfriends or wives thrown in your face or standing in the way of your relationship. Whether their behavior was real or imagined, you want a man who is ready for a new phase in his life.

Here are some common negative statements that should cause you to flee from a man's profile:

- *"I'm not into playing games."*
- *"I'm not looking for anyone with serious baggage."*

- *"My previous girlfriend cheated on me."*
- *"No gold-diggers or liars."*
- *"My difficult divorce..."*
- *"My recent breakup..."*
- *"I was heartbroken..."*
- *"I don't understand why she..."*
- *"Unlike other women I've met..."*

We've all been hurt. We've all had experiences that we would rather have avoided. Hopefully, we have learned from them, processed the lessons and moved through our transitions. *You don't want to be the man's therapist.* If he indicates in his profile that he is newly separated or newly single, think long and hard before you agree to contact him.

My personal rule is to not start anything with a man who is less than two years out of a major breakup.

If your date has been divorced, widowed or ended a long-term relationship less than two years before you meet him, be prepared for the possibility of "baggage" and you will need to spend part of your time facilitating his healing. Or, at the very least, listening to his "war stories".

I've spent my time in the trenches with a newly separated man, and had the stress of hand-holding him through a contentious divorce while I was trying to be thrilled about him being my new boyfriend. It was a schizophrenic existence. Hopefully, you will be wiser than me and try to avoid those men who are newly out on their own, desperate for company while still needing to deal with the bloody mess of a serious breakup. Good luck with that!

Lean towards the man with interesting activities

You don't need to share everything a man does for exercise, education or amusement but it helps to have some activities in common. If he's an avid tennis player and skier, you're going to have a hard time on weekends if you do neither. If he's a pilot or scuba diver, most of these men are happy to find that a novice is interested.

I've dated a man who was a world-class cultivator of bromeliads, a class of plants. I learned a lot about cross-breeding and just being with someone passionate about an unusual activity was invigorating. My girlfriend, Josie, dated a man who collected rare coins. For several months they went to coin shows and gradually fell in love.

Cooking, writing stand-up comedy, playing jazz standards with a group Monday nights, paragliding, raising seeing-eye dogs, gardening, racing sailboats, bicycling, collecting stamps, building a good wine cellar, architectural studies, learning a language or even dressing up in historical costumes—all of these are good green flags that the man writing the profile has depth to his character and is not afraid to explore an interest rather than let it pass.

Don't be turned off by an unusual hobby or worried that he won't have time for you. Welcome the fact that the man has an active mind and imagination that he wants to keep engaged.

Avoid the man who can only think in clichés

Does he "love to walk on the beach?" It must be a very crowded beach. Is he "looking for his soul mate?" Does he want to "spoil you?" Watch out about that last one! But basically, unless you want to be bored, don't choose to contact a man who can only offer the most common over-used clichés.

Not everybody has to be a terrific writer but surely you want some spark of originality in your life. You want some evidence that a new man has that element vital to keeping your life fresh: an imagination.

As you have noticed by now, many men write very limited profile essays. Perhaps they're shy or scared of revealing themselves. Perhaps they're just lazy. In any case, even in the shortest possible essay, look for some sign that the man can express himself with originality. Falling back on tired clichés will only lead you down a tired dead end.

You absolutely need good manners

Any signs that the man is rude should be a signal for you to click away. Being dismissive of any group including political positions, environmentalists, vegetarians, hard-working women, different religions, races or economic classes should be instant deal-breakers.

Any inappropriate sexual comments are red flags

With men over forty, inappropriate, explicit sexual suggestions are not as common as with the outspoken juvenile guys. With my online activity, blatant sexual comments were rare and they were usually pretty tame. (One man praised my dress and wondered what was underneath and another speculated about my breasts. And then I changed my profile photo to a tightly cropped head-shot!)

Be aware that you can flag any inappropriate comments with the site's management and block the user from being able to message you. If you feel the slightest discomfort, do not hesitate to protect yourself. Remember, if you have followed the setup guidelines, you will be safely anonymous, so try not to worry. If you are really concerned, email the site's customer service department and ask for advice.

So, what does it all mean and how you can trust anything you read?

This is where I suggest that you do not agree to meet any man until he has given you his real name and links to third parties where you can get verifiable information. This will be covered in much more detail in *Step 8: Identity: Tips for Learning His True Identity and When Should You Reveal Yours?*

109

Basically, *you should never meet a man without doing research on him.* And, any man who is sincere about the online dating process and is truly interested in meeting you will not object to giving you the information you need to keep yourself safe and prove his truthfulness.

Assuming that you can find out who he is and a considerable amount about his background if you're interested, much of what's written in his profile is subjective. Is he really as witty as he thinks he is? Is he really kind and warm? These are not factual errors but possibly errors in judgment. Remember, it's hard for most people to write an essay pushing their positive qualities and essentially selling themselves. It was hard for you. A little compassion here would go a long way for a man who is just trying to attract you. Now, if he's obnoxious and bragging unnecessarily, that's another matter altogether.

In my experience online, most men over forty are basically truthful and trustworthy about essential facts. Sure, they may shave off a few pounds or a few years, but they don't claim to be dentists if they're really bartenders. Men who are sincere about the online dating process know that women who have read their profiles will be researching their identity and background before meeting them, so their extent of deliberate fudging about factual matters is actually quite small.

Research counts. It's what will keep you from getting caught by a scam artist. It's true that thieves who are trying to talk you out of money are working dating sites with fraudulent stories, and there are more than a few profiles from married men online who are checking out their possibilities. But you can control for these bad apples by demanding information about identity and links to impartial resources like company websites, publications and associations. Facebook links are good. LinkedIn links are even better because his professional reputation is publicly on the line.

I'm an advocate of asking for verifiable links sooner rather than later. If he refuses to give you information you should refuse to continue corresponding with him.

A QUICK CHECKLIST IF YOU'D LIKE TO KEEP SCORE

My friend, Carol, is very methodical and kept a spreadsheet on men she was considering meeting. This is a bit too much for me, but I admire her thoroughness. It paid off, by the way. Carol had very good experiences with the men she met online. Her first dates were unfailingly interesting and well-mannered. It didn't always lead to a second date, but she _always_ had a positive, enjoyable time. After about four months of dating, Carol did meet a wonderful man. They are still happily together.

Carol created a checklist of twelve questions and assigned the prospective man a score of one point for every positive answer. She held to a minimum of score of eight points to consider continuing correspondence and moving towards meeting. If a man had less than eight positive answers, Carol politely extracted herself and said "goodbye."

For more information about red flags and negative answers to watch out for, see the chapter _Know Your List of Potential Deal-Breakers._

Here's Carol's list. Feel free to add questions if you have specific interests. Just make sure that you have at least twelve questions so that the man has a fair chance.

Keep score by adding one point for each question you can answer with "yes". Your best prospective dates should have a score of eight or higher.

Circle each "yes" or "no" answer:

Question#1: Appearance: Did you like his picture? Does he seem appealing? Can you envision yourself standing next to him?	Yes	No
Question #2: Communication: Can he communicate clearly? Is his grammar and spelling acceptable?	Yes	No
Question #3: Does he seem interesting instead of boring? Do the descriptions of his interests and activities indicate a zest for life?	Yes	No
Question #4: Interests in common? Do you share some of his interests or see yourself learning about them? Do his interests excite you?	Yes	No
Question #5: Politics and religion? Are his political and religious views comfortable for you?	Yes	No
Question#6: Education and achievement? Does he match you in levels of education and accomplishment? If he doesn't, are there other factors which make this less important? Is he more educated and accomplished than you? Is this comfortable for you?	Yes	No
Question #7: Optimism? Does he seem to be upbeat and optimistic about his future?	Yes	No

	Yes	No
Question #8: Relationship goals? Does he express the same goals as yours in his search for a relationship?	Yes	No
Question #9: Negativity about past relationships? Is his profile free of complaints about previous relationships or about negative experiences with women in general?	Yes	No
Question #10: Respect for you? Have all of his contacts with you been well-mannered and respectful?	Yes	No
Question #11: Does He show genuine signs of interest? Has he read your profile and made interesting comments on your content? Has he been attentive to subject matter in your email exchanges?	Yes	No
Question #12: Does he work to build your trust? Has he agreed without protest to provide you with his name and links to confirm his identity? Note that a refusal here is a deal-breaker and invalidates all other points!	Yes	No

GRAND TOTALS: YES ____ NO____

Did he pass? Congratulations on finding a man with great potential!

If you are considering meeting a man who has scored at least eight "yes" answers, do your research about him and then arrange a place to meet and an activity you will enjoy. Best wishes for an enjoyable first date and a happy future!

STEP 6
ANSWERING SOMEONE
WHO CONTACTS YOU

Wouldn't it be nice if your perfect man sent you roses and handwritten poems for his first contact? Sadly, most men are even more shy than we are. It takes a self-confident man to write a personal message directly to you on the dating site message board. Most men will just hit the "Wink" or "Poke" button which has no personalized content.

Let's divide the contacts you receive into two groups:

Personalized: Messages that are written just for you. Hooray! This is the strongest expression of interest. A man has sent you an email. You can learn a lot from what he writes and how he writes. It took some effort for him to send you a message. I recommend that you show him the courtesy of writing back, even if it is a quick "thank you, no thank you."

Generic: "Winks," "Pokes," "Pings" or whatever the site calls the automated quick button which sends you a notice expressing his interest. This notice is to let you know that the man has looked at your profile, but it contains no content from him. Whether from shyness or laziness, sending a "wink" requires next to no effort. Your response should also be in the "low-effort" range.

RESPONDING TO GENERIC, NON-PERSONALIZED MESSAGES

Your "Winks" or "Pokes" will outnumber personalized messages ten to one, maybe more. Although this is disappointing, you can move a "Wink" forward by either "Winking" back or writing the first personalized message yourself.

Note that a response to a "Wink" is NOT necessary. You can ignore them unless you're interested in the guy.

- As always, check out the man's profile before making any kind of response.

- If you don't find his profile interesting, delete the "wink" and forget about him.

- If you do like his profile a little bit, send him a "wink" back.

- If you like his profile a lot, write him a quick message.

Keep your message very, very short. Here are two examples of appropriate responses to a "wink":

"Hello through (Dating Site Name)
Thank you for the "wink."
Let me know if you'd like to continue.
Best,
(Your User Name)"

Or:

"Hello through (Dating Site Name)
Thank you for the "wink."
I like your profile, too.
Cheers,
(Your User Name)"

ANSWERING A PERSONALIZED MESSAGE

If a man has gone to the effort of sending you a message with content written expressly for you, I think that you should answer him, even if you are not interested. It's just good manners.

The exception to this rule is if the man is obviously obnoxious or a crank. Never, ever respond to the first email from someone who speaks to you inappropriately. Be sure that you flag him with the site's management. Some sites will allow you to block a sender, also. Then, delete and forget.

Let's assume that the vast majority of your contacts will be good-natured and not cranky. The first thing to do if the message is good-natured is to look at the sender's profile. _Always check out the man's profile before making any kind of response._ Unless his picture is a total turn-off, give the man the benefit of the doubt and read his profile carefully. You may find that you know right away from his writing if you're going to reject him, but if you're not sure, err on the side of potential interest.

Either way, always be polite.

If you're not interested, here's what you can write to answer a personalized message:

> _Thank you for your message. I appreciate you contacting me, but I don't think that we'll be a match. Best of luck with your search!_

If you are interested, use these tips for your first response. Be sure to check out his profile first!

- Write a brief response that includes a reference to something in his profile or something he said in his email. Do not be lengthy. Limit your response to about six sentences, no more.

- Do not offer any additional personal information except, possibly, your first name if he signed his email with his first name.

- Let him know that you're pleased that he contacted you.
- End with an invitation to contact you again.

The first response examples below fall into a pattern. It's useful to have a template to follow. You can expect your second email to be a bit longer and we'll discuss that in a moment. For now, keep your investment of time low—while you are keeping your hopes high.

Hello through OKCupid

I enjoyed your email! Thank you for contacting me.

Your profile touches on so many interesting topics. I especially liked the story about landscaping your garden. I wish my garden stories were as ambitious, but I still spend many happy hours planning and planting.

If you would like to continue, please feel free to contact me again.

Best,
(Your name or user name)

Hello through Match.com

Thank you for contacting me! I enjoyed reading your profile. It seems as though we have many interests in common.

I particularly liked your comments about living abroad and working hard to learn the language. I speak a bit of French, mais oui…but it's a struggle and I wish I knew more. Trips to France are always at the top of my wish list!

If you would like to continue, I'd be happy to hear from you again.

Au revoir,
(Your name or user name)

Hello through EHarmony

Thank you for your email. I have read your profile with interest and would enjoy getting to know you.

What you wrote about loving to cook caught my attention. Last week, I took a class in Thai cooking. It was a pleasure to learn about new ingredients and I'm looking forward many delicious meals practicing with them. Do you like to take cooking classes?

Let me know if you'd like to continue.

Best regards,
(Your name or user name)

Hello through PlentyofFish

Your email made me laugh out loud with your snowboarding story. Thank you so much for contacting me.

I've read your profile with interest. It seems as though we have many activities in common. In addition to winter sports, I'm particularly interested in your work with city planning since you know from my profile that I'm an architect. How long have been in your own practice?

Please feel free to contact me again. I look forward to hearing from you.

Cheers,
(Your name or user name)

Being brief but expressing your interest directly is a good way to keep the correspondence going. If you are especially interested, include a question or two. Be careful about answering questions or writing a long, revealing email. You haven't had the chance to research the man yet—you need his name to do this. You will ask for it in your next cycle.

You've completed one message cycle but you haven't heard back from him

It's possible that the man has sent out lots and lots of messages, has become interested in exchanging emails with another woman. He may be ignoring some of his contacts. If you are really interested, just check in with him gently.

> *Hi there*
> *We exchanged messages last week but I haven't heard back from you. Are you interested in continuing?*
> *Thanks,*
> *(Your name or user name)*

You have completed one message cycle and now you're launched into a correspondence

Congratulations! You have a new potential friend. If you are a strong correspondent already, you won't need much guidance here except to review the goals below. If you are more of the Twitter-one-hundred-and-forty-characters type of writer, that's good too. Basically, you should move away now from any templates or formula, relax and just be yourself.

3 IMPORTANT GOALS WHEN ESTABLISHING EMAIL CORRESPONDENCE

Don't lose sight of your overall purpose: to manage your online dating experience sensibly, efficiently, enjoyably, safely and for the best possible outcome. You may be excited to have started a personalized correspondence with a man with great potential. Don't lose your head. Stay grounded and sensible by paying attention to the following three goals.

Goal #1: Learn his true name: The sooner you learn the man's real name, the sooner you will be able to research him online. At the earliest opportunity, you want to verify the truth of what he has presented in his profile and also confirm that he is a responsible, trustworthy citizen.

Hopefully, if the guy is interested in meeting you, he will already have offered contact information. If not, you can ask. See also the whole chapter *Step 8: Identity: Tips for Learning His True Identity and When Should You Reveal Yours?*

I can't stress enough what a potential waste of time it is to continue emailing with a man whose true identity is unknown.

Goal #2: Learn about his spontaneous thought process: Casual, written correspondence is a good indicator of someone's thought process. Learn as much as you can from his second email.

I say "casual" because the man presumably put some time and effort into writing his profile, just like you did. It was an edited work, done in a controlled environment. Once you move to spontaneous messages, that framework is gone and there's a lot more you can learn about his personality.

Take notes about how he observes the world. Is he optimistic? Do you see clues of depression? Do you see clues of anger about previous relationships? Has he expanded on what he likes to do and would see doing with you? Are you comfortable and genuinely interested in those activities? Does he feel like his career matters to him (or mattered, if he's retired) and he is making a positive difference in the world? Is he a worry-wart? Is he politically opposed to your values or does he share your world views about what would be good solutions to the major problems the planet is facing.

It's time to move away from just small talk. Ask questions but don't pry. Keep them focused AWAY from past relationships. Do not ask what happened with his ex-wife and do not get drawn into correspondence that focuses on learning from past mistakes.

You want a FRESH START with associations that are only about you. Keep only two people in your messages: you and him. Leave the ex-wives, ex-husbands and frustrating first dates out of your correspondence.

Goal #3: Make a hard decision as soon as you can about whether you want to meet this man then move forward as soon as possible: To someone who doesn't have experience with Internet dating, this probably sounds like a risky, crazy suggestion. But, I am a big believer in meeting sooner rather than later.

Long email trails are fine if you want a pen pal. If you want a warm-blooded date, your goal should be to use as few email cycles as possible to move the two of you towards meeting face-to-face. After you have done your research on him and checked him out, of course!

Here are five very good reasons why you want to meet as soon as possible:

First, most obviously, if you are looking for a relationship, you need to check out the physical chemistry. Sure, there are stories about men and women who emailed for a year, fell in love and lived happily ever after. Personally, I don't know anybody who started a serious relationship this way. For the most of us, we should treat this story as an Urban Myth.

Second, there are lifestyle elements that can be concealed in emails that become very obvious in person. For example, I was interested in a wonderful, smart man whose profile concealed the fact that he's in a wheelchair. Sensibly from his part, he was looking for a woman who would fall in love with his essence and not be turned away by the realities of him being a paraplegic. I sympathized with him, but this was not my destiny. If I had been in love with him, then, of course, I would have stayed by his side. But I wasn't prepared to start a relationship as a caregiver.

Third, your overall goal in online dating is to have an enjoyable time with the whole process. You do not want a built-in structure of disappointment. The more you invest in corresponding with the guy, the more disappointed you will be if he turns out to be a dud. Keep the ratio of your investment to expectations in balance! Prepare to be pleasantly surprised if you genuinely like him in person and don't build up a "head of steam" or overblown fantasies over weeks of emailing back and forth. Letting your imagination run wild is a natural reaction to a long email correspondence, but you do not want to live in a fantasy world. Guard against this.

Fourth, sad to say but there are money-scammers who are using online dating to talk women out of money. Imagine this scenario: some wonderful-sounding guy contacts you, hooks you into correspondence and then has a financial crisis. He needs help. Please send $5,000 to help him rebuild his apartment in New Jersey that was damaged in Hurricane Sandy. The only problem is that this guy is really in Indonesia and has twenty or thirty vulnerable, needy single women on his hook. Beware! Moving towards suggesting a meeting will knock these scammers right out of the water. Never, ever, ever send money to a man you have "met" online. You haven't really met him. He isn't really your soul mate. He's a thief.

Fifth, it's also very sad to say that there are an unknown number of married men who surf online dating sites, especially free ones like OKCupid and PlentyofFish. (If they signed up for a paid site, the monthly charge would show up on their charge card records.) If you ask for his true name and he refuses, this is a pretty strong clue. If he has provided his name and you suggest meeting in a public place and he refuses, that's also a strong message.

A lot of this information is going to be repeated in the chapters that follow and I'll use those chapters to make an even stronger case for meeting sooner rather than later. This approach has really worked for me and it can work for you, too! You can turn a series of dull, disappointing first dates into an enjoyable series of evenings out that you will look back on as time well-spent.

After all, the single most important thing we all have to offer is our time. Don't waste your precious time by emailing men who turn out to be dead ends.

STEP 7
HOW TO INITIATE CONTACT
WITH A MAN ONLINE

Most women feel shy or awkward about reaching out to email a man before he contacts them. Don't you think that this is a holdover from our traditional mandate that a man is supposed to make the first contact? Many people don't feel comfortable promoting themselves, mostly because they haven't had the practice. Acknowledging these feelings of shyness and discomfort is important and you can get past this and learn to be a pro-active participant online!

Don't be held back. Confidence comes with practice.

It's a new world out there with online dating. If you take the passive position and wait for contacts to come to you, your experience will be diminished because you will be eliminating the greatest source of activity: you! If you want to meet men and have lots of first dates to maximize your opportunities, you must be active and do your share of the heavy lifting. You must learn to reach out and contact a man first.

You don't have to get over being shy or feeling awkward. You just need the tools to be able to proceed anyway. _What you really need is courage to change your life_, and the faith that with practice, you will be able to email a man online and it won't be painful. It will be fun!

YOU WROTE YOUR PROFILE, NOW PROMOTE IT

To continue the theme that putting up your profile is like launching a personal brand, you can logically see the next step: promotion. This is "Sales and Marketing" by a more gracious name. Anyone who has worked in marketing knows that you cannot invent a product and hope it will sell without any promotion. You must broadcast the news to prospective clients.

The dating sites that have good algorithms for matching people will do some promotion for you when they create matches. You can put matching criteria into a general search at any time, or you can depend on the automatic searches that some sites provide. (OKCupid has a "Quiver" with three quick matches that they send automatically. You then rate their choices and the algorithms learn your preferences.)

But...except for the matching functions, the dating sites are not going to promote you! It's very important to realize this because the ball is absolutely in your court to take action if you want positive results. To mix the metaphors, dating sites basically provide the dance floor for the party. You can chose to stand against the wall like a wallflower, or you can move towards the center of the floor and into the spotlight.

This is all under your control. You are the designer of your experience. The dating sites will give you a nudge forward with the match lists but it is up to you to take action.

Here's what I did: OKCupid has a function that allows you to see who visited your profile. Every time I checked in online, I took a look. (Remember—there will always be more viewers when you first go online because most sites have another function that identifies "Who's New.") I looked carefully at the men who had viewed me. Unless their photos were a total turn-off, I returned the favor and looked at their profiles.

If I thought that there was any possibility that the man would be an interesting first date, I sent him a quick message.

Hello through OKCupid

Thank you for visiting my profile! I see from reading yours that we have interests in common.

Please let me know if you'd like to continue.

Best regards
Christie

The perils of applying too much judgment

So, you're looking a guy's profile and the voices in your head are raging about how he's just not right. He isn't educated enough. He doesn't have a prestigious-enough career. His grooming looks sloppy. OK. Possibly that's all true. And, maybe there will be a spectacular man online who satisfies all your fantasies. He's probably there, somewhere, just waiting to contact you.

But maybe he won't contact you. Maybe you need to contact him first.

Is this you? You will need practice in contacting men. You need to get out and go on some first dates. You're lonely. You're frustrated. You're tired of going everywhere alone or with girlfriends. The profile you're reading isn't that of a perfect man, but the odds are that meeting him would be an interesting evening for you—certainly more interesting than staying at home watching reruns of Downton Abbey. He's probably a decent guy with similar hopes and dreams. And...the odds of him being an ax murderer are miniscule. He might actually be worried about the same dangers from you!

You're not choosing a husband. You're moving towards choosing a first date.

Let's try *not* to throw all of your selection requirements at the poor guy at the first glance. It's true that the process of dating is a process of elimination. But, again, you need the practice. (Not to forget your authentic deal-breakers. For a fresher, review the chapter *Know Your List of Potential Deal-Breakers.*)

There is a difference between legitimate practice and completely wasting your time. Be open to practice, but obviously, don't waste your time.

Remember, also, that I am not a fan of going for coffee on your first date. My very strong recommendation is that you chose an activity that you would like to do but don't want to do alone. Like a concert, a music club, a museum opening, a lecture or a wine and cheese festival. Something that is public, safe for you and interesting. I will be stressing this strategy for first dates over and over again in this book. Coffee is boring. Doing something you like is interesting. And—here's the important part—it takes the pressure off the man to be stellar. He can be ordinary. He can even be a total dud. You've still had an interesting evening.

Ultimately, it's all about taking control. You control with whom you are in contact by initiating the contact. You control your activity for the first date by planning ahead and suggesting an interesting activity. You control the quality of your experience by moving towards being the manager.

Be the CEO of your dating life. Be confident.

SAMPLE EMAILS YOU CAN USE TO INITIATE THE FIRST CONTACT

If you are reaching out to send the first email, it's really very simple. Don't be shy about using an email like these examples. You'll see how simple and short these message are. They are easy and quick to send.

Outreach Email #1: Invite him to visit your profile

You've looked at his profile carefully and you are interested in him. He has not contacted you yet. You gather up your courage and take sixty seconds to send him this quick message:

Hello through OKCupid

I've read your profile and think that we have interests in common. When you have a moment, please take a look at my profile and see if you agree.

Best wishes,
(Your user name or first name)

Or:

Hello through Match.com

I enjoyed reading your profile and hope that you would enjoy looking at mine. Please take a look and let me know if you'd like to continue.

Best wishes,
(Your user name or first name)

Outreach Email #2: Thank him for visiting your profile

He has been a visitor to your profile and you've looked at his. You're interested in continuing. You wonder why he didn't send you a message or "Wink" at you but you still gather up your courage and take sixty seconds to send him this quick message:

Hello through OKCupid

Thank you for visiting my profile. I've read yours and think that we have interests in common. Would you like to continue?

Best wishes,
(Your name or user name)

Or:

Hello through Match.com

Thank you for visiting my profile. I enjoyed reading yours and see that we have a lot in common. Would you like to continue?

Best wishes,
(Your name or user name)

It's common advice to include a reference to something actually in his profile, but I think you can leave that out. Here's why: trying to pick something personal to say will both slow you down and make you anxious. At least, it makes me anxious. I worry about the choice then worry about how I am going to make note of it in a first short email. I think you can err on the side of being comfortable and leave it out personal references. Keep the first email generic.

If the man is interested, he will get back to you. Or, at the very least, if he's polite he will get back to you, regardless of the level of his interest.

Assuming that his response is positive, you're launched! You can refer to *Step 6 Answering A Man Who Contacts You* for tips on how to proceed from here.

Why being passive will lead to a mediocre experience and empty evenings. It's easy this to change this!

Are you in your own black hole? Do you look forward to evening after evening alone? It doesn't need to be that way, but you are the only one who can change your experience. A mythical white knight is not going to show up on your doorstep.

You are the action hero in your own story. As you can see from the email examples above, it doesn't take a lot of action to get something going.

Here's what you can do to create action: *Commit to sending one new email a day to a man who has NOT contacted you.* Just one email per man. Not multiple emails. Send a first, short email as a feeler to find out his interest. If he doesn't respond, no matter. Tomorrow, you will send another to a different man. And the day after, another.

Soon, you will have a management problem: how to schedule the first dates and what activities will you do? Again, no coffee dates! Plan ahead and think about what you'd like to do. Even browsing through a bookstore together is more interesting than sitting over coffee.

Interesting activities are the alternative to sitting alone. All you need to do is commit to being brave enough to reach out and make the first contact.

BUILD YOUR CONFIDENCE WITH THESE TIPS

Were you the shy one in school who was afraid to raise her hand in class? Me, too. But you aren't going to be graded on your performance with online dating.

Here are six confidence builders that will help you be comfortable when you reach out to contact a man first:

Tip #1: Put the effort into your profile: Give creating your profile your best positive effort. When you know that your profile is well-written, your photographs are good and the overall presentation reflects the best of you, you can be relaxed and proud to promote it. You will feel that you have presented yourself on solid ground. You will be confident and have no need to second guess what you have published.

Tip #2: Do your homework when learning how to decode a man's profile: Before you contact anyone, get some practice looking at pictures and reading essays. Be aware of your reactions. Know what you really like, what you really dislike and what you could be prepared to ignore.

Tip #3: Keep the models of first emails handy for your reference: You shouldn't have to scramble or be anxious, wondering what to say. Make the whole process as easy and smooth as possible by being prepared to just write and send. It's important to plan and prepare before you write. That way, the writing is just rote activity. No anxiety. Just do it.

Tip #4: Trust that you have taken all practical safety precautions: Take my suggestions for keeping yourself safe and protecting your true identity seriously. You will find specific information in *Step 1: Getting Ready.* If you have protected your identity, you will be writing to men anonymously. Just enjoy the process.

Tip #5: Plan ahead for the possibility of the man's response: Know what kind of activities you would like to do on a first date. Be prepared to move forward by knowing what you will say—and what you will NOT say—in any subsequent email exchanges.

Tip #6: And finally, relax: You are not choosing a husband or life-partner. You're just sending a three sentence email. Anonymously. It may never come to more than that. If it does, great, but don't drive yourself crazy with unrealistic expectations before anything happens. It's just an email. You will send lots of them.

Don't exhaust yourself by getting worked up over the first few emails. Remember, this is a project with a long-term timeline. Pace yourself by being practical and realistic. Be ready to enjoy the process, knowing that you have the skills to be proactive and to be in control.

STEP 8

IDENTITY: TIPS FOR LEARNING HIS TRUE IDENTITY AND WHEN SHOULD YOU REVEAL YOURS?

You should never meet a man in person before checking him out with multiple online resources. To do this, you need to get behind his username and learn his real name as soon as you've realized that you would like to meet him.

In my case, I usually had a pretty good idea if I wanted to meet the man by the second or third email. That's when I asked for his name, if he hadn't already volunteered it. Below are sample emails that you can use to ask for his name and other identity verification information.

With his real name, you can do a Google web search and follow the links. Don't forget to search Google Images, too, and follow the relevant links there. You can also look on LinkedIn and Facebook. There's a list at the end of this chapter with more details.

These days, researching someone isn't hard, especially if he is over forty. If he is a professional with a company profile, it's especially easy to confirm his identity. If he's a published author, a faculty member, an award winner, an athlete, an entertainer or just a good, solid citizen involved with volunteer groups, there is probably an Internet trail of his activities, just as there would be of yours.

If you really want to get serious about research, there's a useful website that is used by millions of people called www.beenverified.com. You can sign up for a three month membership and do unlimited background checks. This company makes it easy for online daters. They even have a category called "Social Searches."

In all my online dating experience, only one man on JDate refused to give me his name after I asked politely. He claimed to be worried that I was a stalker. Don't bother wasting any more time on someone like this. He's either flat-out crazy or, more likely, married and trying to hide that he is sniffing around other women. Hit the delete button. Quickly.

Most men WANT to meet a good woman and will be happy to do whatever they can to make you feel comfortable. I've even had guys send me a picture of their driver's license!

Researching has become a normal part of the online dating process. Today, men understand that you need to check them out in order to feel comfortable meeting in person. Most men I found online were very co-operative and understanding. I hope this is your experience, too.

SAMPLE EMAILS TO ASK
FOR HIS REAL NAME

It's not hard to learn his true identity once you realize that you can just ask. The man expects you to. No man who is respectful of women would be surprised that you want to keep yourself safe and any respectful man will support your efforts. Just be matter-of-fact. Don't sound paranoid. Sound practical.

Here's the email I used, time and time again:

Hello again

I've enjoyed our emails and hope we are moving forward towards meeting.

My young adult children are nervous about their mom meeting men online. How's that for role reversal?! They insist that I check you out. Would you feel comfortable sending me your full name and links to any website like your company profile, publications or organizations? Thanks for doing this. I'm sure you understand.

Best,
Christie

If you feel comfortable, you can offer to exchange names. Here's another email I used which always got results:

Hi Charles

Yes, I'm interested in continuing to get to know you! Thanks for your email.

Since I hope we could meet sometime soon, would you feel comfortable sending me your full name? If you have any links to your professional profile or other websites with information about you, that would be great, too. I'm sure you understand that I feel more comfortable doing a little research before we meet.

Just to be fair, I'll be happy to send you my full name, too. You can Google me for more information.

Best,
Christie

WHEN SHOULD YOU REVEAL YOUR IDENTITY?

Only someone who genuinely understands your comfort level could advise you on when to reveal your true identity. There are so many variables, especially for single women. If you have a trusted friend or family member, therapist or anyone else who knows you well and cares about your sense of safety, talking about how open you should be with strange men online would be a good discussion to have before you put up your profile.

Of course, the person who best understands your comfort level is you!

Note how the way I formed the sentence above can shift your attitude: "strange men online." Uh oh! The bogeyman. Scary, scary. Note also that we're talking about "your sense of safety" not your actual safety. They are different, obviously, but both are important for how comfortable and enjoyable you will find the online dating process.

Statistically, you are not in greater danger from a stranger online than you are from a stranger you meet in person at a singles' event. By far, the majority of men are peaceful, trustworthy and intend you no harm. That said, there is a small percentage of men who *are* physically abusive or will try to take your money or are in some other way dangerous to be around. We all hope to avoid men like this in our social lives, in our families, in our workplace and in our communities.

There are no trustworthy statistics that will give you the odds of meeting a dangerous guy. Two out of one hundred? One out of one thousand? No one really knows. Just as there are dangerous drivers on the road, there are dangerous men looking to prey on women on the Internet. It's simply a fact of life for which you need to be careful.

Note that I said "careful," not "paranoid."

What can you do to avoid that 2% or 0.2%? Do your research! Run a background check! If you can't find positive information about a man online, don't meet him. Don't reveal your identity until your research confirms that this man is someone you could feel comfortable meeting and introducing to your friends.

Another important point is to be trustworthy yourself. I've taken the position that the women who read this book are upstanding citizens. Honest, even-tempered and open-minded. But the reality could be very different. Men sometimes complain that women online just want to go out for a free meal. (This is another reason why I believe that "going Dutch" is the best policy.) And we all saw that horror movie *Fatal Attraction* about a casual date with a woman who turned out to be a stalker nightmare.

So, it's simply the truth that both men and women have reason to be cautious. And it's also true that you can be optimistic that the person you connect with online will be a sincere and trustworthy man who you'll enjoy getting to know.

RESOURCES FOR DOING BACKGROUND CHECKS

The best place to start is with a web search on Google: www.google.com.

Follow the links. If he's a professional, you will probably find a LinkedIn profile. www.LinkedIn.com. If you have a LinkedIn profile yourself, you can have access to his basic information. If you don't, it's free to set up. Pay particular attention to the groups listed at the bottom of his profile page. Groups must approve the use of their logo, so this is verified information.

Try a search using Google images: www.google.com/images. This is much more haphazard as it's not as well filtered. Under the image there are links to follow. Be careful because there are usually many people with the same name.

Facebook is an obvious resource: www.facebook.com. Do a quick search to see if his picture matches up with what he posted on the dating site. Many younger women insist that a potential date "friend" them on Facebook. This way, they have access to so much information about the guy. I have a Facebook profile but have never done this. Actually, I would resist since I wouldn't want a stranger have access to my friends, but maybe it's just because I'm older and less comfortable with Facebook. Think about it and make the choice that's comfortable for you.

If he has provided you with a link to his company profile, that's golden. Go to the webpage and read every word.

You can use fee-based websites that do background checks if you can afford it. My favorite is www.beenverified.com. Membership with them entitles you to unlimited searches that can verify contact information, credit history and any criminal record. As of this writing, a year's membership fee is $96. Three months membership is $48. It seems like money well spent for your peace of mind.

Another fee-based background check website is www.peoplewise.com which charges a fee for each search. $1.95 or $2.95 won't get you as much information as their premium search for $25.95, but if you're really concerned, this is where to go. Peoplewise is part of www.lexisnexis.com, the powerful website specializing in risk management.

STEP 9
GETTING READY TO DATE

Should you meet the man you've been emailing? A better question might be *"why not meet him?"* There are many reasons to resist moving off the safety and comfort of staying online. The safety concerns are obvious. Less obvious is that your emotional exposure is limited. Even if you are already emotionally engaged with the man online, if no one sees you, it's your private matter. Rejection is so much more intense in person. And...happily...so is attraction.

Deciding to meet is a pivotal choice and deserves serious consideration.

There are two basic ways you can approach meeting a man you've found online: the first way is to rely on the romantic fantasy that you will meet your soul-mate, thanks to the magic of a dating site's matching abilities. Of course, this can happen! People contact each other online every day and fall in love when they meet.

This is the model that is advertised by the big dating sites. The problem is that it really puts a lot of pressure on you to make each first date into a marriage interview. Even if that's your goal, it's unrealistic to think that lightning will strike on your first date. And, expecting that every subsequent first date will lead to Something Big is a recipe for feeling pressured and anxious. Not to mention the disappointment and discouragement that you will feel each time the hoped for magic doesn't work out.

Why not be more comfortable? It's more realistic to understand that you will need to meet several men—maybe even dozens of men—before you find one who lights up your heart and sends sparks flying.

This takes the pressure off any one date. You could even think about meeting a man just because he might be a pleasant companion for an activity. Maybe you don't need to pre-qualify every man as a potential husband. Maybe you could just go out and meet someone new and do something interesting together. And, when you are practiced and relaxed about going out and know how to enjoy yourself in this rather awkward 21st Century world of Internet dating, eventually you will meet someone special.

That's the second way to approach meeting men you've found online: being realistic that you will need to experience many first dates and you deserve to have a good time while you're doing them.

Let's take a look at what you can do to prepare making the process enjoyable.

SHIFT YOUR ATTITUDE: HOW TO MANAGE FIRST DATES LIKE A MULTI-PHASE PROJECT, NOT ISOLATED EVENTS

If you're adding online dating to your life in any kind of serious way then it helps to shift your attitude: *Instead of thinking about each date as an isolated activity, consider dating as an over-all project with many episodes.*

If you meet a wonderful man on one of your early dates, so much the better. But, realistically, if you are prepared to go on many first dates, you will have more success controlling the quality of your experience because you will be managing these dates as a series. Project management skills are very useful here!

Your goal, then, should be to make the overall first date as interesting and enriching as possible. That way, when you look back over your time, say over six months or twelve months, you will feel good about what you've been doing.

Treating dating as a Grand Project has many advantages including:

- It helps takes immediate pressure off any single date so you can relax and enjoy yourself more at that particular time.

- You will have the confidence to believe that there will be many first dates so any one dating flop isn't such a burden. If you follow the rules below about how to choose your date activity, you will have a good time anyway, even if the guy is a dud.

- You will gain perspective. Feeling overly invested in any one date can be self-defeating. And it can make you anxious-crazy in the process. Dating should be entertaining and fun! By accepting that a single date is part of a larger whole, you can be more effective when it comes to adjusting your strategies for having a pleasant time overall.

Prepare what you need ahead of time: Don't let yourself scramble at the last minute

Well-managed projects that include repeated actions will make those actions as efficient as possible. Think about what you can do with _one_ preparation that could be used over and over for multiple dates. This will save you time and the stress of last minute decisions.

Here are three things to prepare in anticipation:

Preparation Tip #1: Clothing: Know what you're going to wear. Don't scramble at the last minute looking for something to wear. Put together two or three basic first date outfits. Choose one for day and one for night. Select jewelry, accessories and shoes. If you can, put them together in your closet so getting ready is an easy, one-stop preparation. If that's not practical, make notes on how to combine the outfits and keep that page of notes in your closet where you can easily find it.

Whenever possible, avoid stress just before you go out on a first date. Do you fret about what to wear? Trying on different outfits at the last minute can be confidence-destroyer. Don't do this to yourself! Better to have a pre-chosen winning outfit that you will feel great wearing.

Preparation Tip #2: Safety Monitors: Just like having a designated driver if you're out drinking, you need a designated person who knows that you're out on a first date. Set this up ahead of time so you're not wondering who to call at the last minute. Know who you are going to tell about where you will be and with whom. Leave all the contact information you have about the first date like his name and cell phone number. Then, be sure to contact your friend when you return safely so s/he can go off Red Alert!

Preparation Tip #3: Brainstorm a list of activities you'd like to do: This is your chance to re-invent your life. What would you like to do if you had one or two hours with a companion? Be as imaginative as you can! Of course you need to be practical about distance, but surely there are things to do in your hometown that are more interesting than going for coffee.

With a list ready to go, you can make suggestions to your first date that will not only please you but will also demonstrate to him that you are a creative person with whom to spend quality time. Most people do not plan ahead. When _you_ do, you will stand out from the crowd. Be the leader here and you will get what you want.

There's much more information on finding activities below in this chapter. Plus, see the chapter _10 Great Activities for First Dates_. Also, in _Step 10: Creating Enjoyable First Dates_ there are sample emails you can use to invite the man to the activity of your choice. There's guidance to help you do this every step of the way!

WHY SKIPPING THE "TELEPHONE INTERVIEW" CAN BE A GOOD IDEA

Are you absolutely certain that you need to conduct a "telephone interview" before you agree to meet a man? In my experience, it can be a better choice to skip the "telephone interview" and go straight to meeting in person.

You have already decoded the man's profile and have been exchanging emails. What's next? Somewhere along the line it became the normal pattern to talk on the phone before you agree to meet in person. I say _"forget this!"_ I went on numerous first dates without a prior "telephone interview" and never regretted it. When my date and I met for the first time, it was usually the first time I heard his voice. Sometimes I was surprised. Most of the time, pleasantly.

The first telephone calls are awkward for everybody. It's a rare individual who can talk smoothly and sound great, and a rare first phone conversation that is enjoyable and comfortable for both of you. And, most importantly, after the call, you won't have any more answers about his physical attractiveness, his personal habits, or if there's any chemistry between you.

Early on in my dating process, I went along with the "phone first, meet later" philosophy and then I decided to drop the call. Here's why: for most first dates, we have one shot. Only one chance at contact. And sometimes it's not him that's doing the rejecting. You could easily decide that this isn't a guy with whom you'd like to spend more time. By the time you've researched any man you're choosing to meet, you can feel pretty confident that the two of you will be well-mannered and behave appropriately for a first visit in a public place.

Why waste your first and possibly only shot for companionship with him on a phone call? With most of my phone calls, lightning didn't strike and I was at best lukewarm about the man. If the result is that he's not a keeper, why not meet to do something that you've been wanting to do instead of sitting at home alone? You will come to the place separately and leave separately. And, in between, you will have an interesting time during which, hopefully, you will be meeting a wonderful man. Even if he's a dud, you _still_ have had the interesting time to add good memories to your life by enjoying the activity. (See _Step 10: Creating Enjoyable First Dates_ for lots of suggestions about this!)

Meeting to see each other's body language and all the information that face-to-face contact provides is SUCH A BETTER USE OF YOUR TIME than a phone call. The "telephone interview" is a waste of a good opportunity for companionship and information gathering.

"It takes more time to meet than to call," you say. True, but if you have planned ahead, preparing for the first date will be smooth. Plus, you will get to do something more memorable than talking with a stranger on the phone.

You can make all your arrangements by email. You can even exchange long, information-filled emails.

It's just convention and tradition which says that you proceed from a profile to an email to a phone call...then to a personal meeting. I disagree with this tradition and avoided the phone call portion on most of my first dates.

And, guess what! 100% of the men I dated were happy to skip the telephone call, too. I never had a man say _"Stop!_

Wait! We need to have a phone call first!" Most men feel just as awkward as we do meeting a stranger. Most men are also tired of going places alone or with male friends.

Let's plan for your success. Skip the phone call whenever you can and go straight to the in-person meeting.

WHO PAYS FOR THE FIRST DATE? LET'S TALK ABOUT MONEY!

Meeting for coffee or a glass of wine is the classic first date for online singles. It's easy to arrange and inexpensive. Traditionally, the man pays for the date's expenses because men have traditionally been the money earners and controlled most financial decisions. Fifty years ago, this might have been the norm but it seems old fashioned today. Today, even well into the 21st Century, many dating advisors insist that the proper arrangement for your first date is that the man always pays. It's like we never left the 1950's.

Many women still feel shy talking about money, despite that fact that most women understand the value of financial independence. Forty percent of American wives earn more than their husbands; yet, after they divorce, when it comes to dating it somehow isn't polite or acceptable for the woman to offer to pay her own expenses.

You'd think that offering $10 or $20 towards an activity more interesting than going for coffee was some kind of disease to be avoided by well-bred women hoping to meet well-bred men. In fact, this is a social anachronism. It's limiting to be stuck in dating protocols from days gone by. Don't you think it's time to stake your claim to the 21st Century?

Please consider the case for offering to "go Dutch" and paying your own expenses on your first date. Whatever you arrange *after* the first date is up to you! Maybe in old etiquette books it was the end of the world if a woman had to touch money but I think "going Dutch" will open a whole new world of possibilities for you.

Here's why: being willing to contribute $10 or $20 towards your first date expenses broadens your choices to include so many enjoyable activities beyond just going for coffee. Plus, you will stand out from the crowd as a resourceful woman who is willing to invest in the time the two of you spend together. Your date will appreciate your thoughtfulness!

In *Step 10: Creating Enjoyable First Dates* you will find sample emails to help you offer "going Dutch" in a comfortable way. You will find, like I did, that men are thrilled to be released from the repetition of meeting for coffee. They will be grateful and eager to meet you.

If you refuse to contribute financially, your first dates will most likely be limited to low-cost, ordinary activities like meeting in a coffee house. You could be lucky enough to meet a Silicon Valley billionaire who flies you off to Hawaii for a Kona coffee, but let's be realistic and keep our feet on the ground.

If you insist that the man pay for everything you do together before you even know each other, you won't do much. Why not? If the man *always* pays, it's a practical choice for him to keep dating expenses very low. He's minimizing his risk. The guy you're meeting is no dummy. He knows that he'll be meeting twenty or thirty women or more. He might even be worried that some women just want an evening out and aren't sincerely interested in him. That's happened and men do talk about wasting money when they discuss dating, just like women talk about their experiences.

So, here's your chance to stand out from the crowd and create an opportunity to do something special for your first date: offer "going Dutch" to an interesting activity.

Prepare to enrich your life: Do something interesting on your first dates

There's a big, wide wonderful world out there beyond the coffee shop. Plus, many of the places where you and your date can meet are free or very low cost. Some take an hour, some longer. How much time you want to spend with the man can be part of your activity choice. Consider how much more interesting your first dates will be if you:

- Meet in the lobby of a museum. See an exhibit, then go for a cappuccino in the museum cafe if things are going well. Most museums are open late one night a week. If you're a member, it's a free visit for both of you. If neither of you has membership, the admission fee is $10—$20. Plus, you'll see what he looks like dressed up!

- Meet at the front door of a jazz club, cabaret or music club. You can buy tickets at the door ($15—$25) and have at least 30 minutes to visit before the concert. If it's going well, have a drink later. If the date is a dud, you've at least had a companion to go someplace you might not feel comfortable going alone.

- Meet at a book store and browse the aisles together. It's free and interesting. For readers, this is always a good way to spend an hour.

- Take a cooking class together ($35) if you both love to cook. You'll need to sign up in advance. Check out your local community center or upscale kitchen supply store for their schedule.

- Support your local theater group by going to a performance. Meet in the lobby. Small theater often is surprisingly inexpensive ($12—$20) and enjoyable.

- Sign up for www.Goldstar.com for access to half-price tickets for many premium events like symphonies and the theater. After he has committed to the event, you'll need to agree who actually buys the tickets with the promise of reimbursement. I bought the tickets for about half of my first dates and the man either bought dinner or paid me back. I was NEVER stood up on a first date.

- Walk through a summer Art and Wine Festival. Free.
- Meet on campus at your local college for a concert or lecture ($10—$20). If you're lucky enough to live near a big college, there are multiple offerings. Put your name on their email newsletter to receive notifications.

On my dozens of first dates, only one man insisted on meeting for coffee and refused any activity I offered. He turned out to be duller than dirt. In every other case, when I made suggestions for activities, the man was grateful and happily agreed. The result was that we went to jazz concerts, symphony concerts, multiple museums, festivals and many wonderful theater performances. If I hadn't asked, I would have just had dozens of cups of coffee.

I loved my experiences of first dates and you can have a great time, too! All you need is a go-to list of activities that interest you, be willing to pay for your own admission and have the courage to ask!

Some women have an easier time than others taking the initiative, but even if you're shy and feel awkward, you will find that this gets easier with practice. And, as soon as you've had a couple of first dates made memorable thanks to your improved choice of activities, you will never go back to the boring and unimaginative default of *"Let's meet for coffee."*

Your dates will be grateful, too.

BECOMING COMFORTABLE SUGGESTING ACTIVITIES

Leadership takes many forms. Traditionally, the woman waits passively for a man to make all the social overtures to which she politely responds. The man is expected to be the leader. Even when I was a teenager, the thought of calling a boy before he called me was truly horrifying. But is this really the best way to guarantee yourself an enjoyable experience as a woman going back into the "dating scene" when you're over forty years old? Do we really need to do everything the way our mothers and grandmothers did?

When it comes to online dating and enjoying a series of first dates that might stretch out over many months, taking responsibility for the quality of your time is the best way to guarantee that you will enjoy yourself.

You're capable and probably have a very good idea of what kind of activities you'd like to do. And if not, this is your opportunity to explore doing new things! You may be very experienced at arranging events or you may have spent years arranging the social life for your children. Maybe you're a little rusty organizing your own social life as a single woman so it's a scary process. I was nervous myself when I started reaching out on the Internet.

In *Step 10: Creating Enjoyable First Dates* there is step-by-step guidance on how to write email invitations that will be well received. You will have positive results!

Taking the initiative works really well for online dating. But don't take the position that you are the only decision maker—that planning a meeting is "your way or the highway". Nobody likes a pushy person. Make suggestions, not demands. You will find that most men are delighted that you care about making time together enjoyable. They're bored with coffee dates, too!

BUILDING A SOCIAL CALENDAR

Here's how my friend, Carolyn, invented her social life. You can use her methods to jump-start your social calendar. Carolyn is a whirlwind of energy. She's sixty-three, retired, divorced and her children are grown. She has free hours but not a lot of extra money. She wanted to meet a man and fall in love. Carolyn said that she is tired of going places alone and coming home to an empty house.

Carolyn set out to invent a social life that would provide her with a stream of interesting activities, meet new people and, hopefully, find romance. She started looking around her community and discovered that most organizations have websites with free newsletters and event notices. She signed up to a variety of newsletters and put her email on the mailing lists of interesting groups. It didn't happen overnight but soon Carolyn's inbox was full of invitations and announcements for events.

She also invested about $200 in memberships that required annual dues. She became a member at two local museums and joined nature clubs. For music and theater, she signed up for free newsletters that announce performances. Soon, it was no effort at all to find interesting things to do on weekends, evenings and during the weekday. She scanned the newsletters and announcements and just made notes on her calendar. That way, Carolyn knew her schedule could be filled with things to look forward to. And, if she wanted to invite a friend, the information was easy to find.

A social calendar is a wonderful asset. Whether you make entries on your smart phone or on a paper calendar, seeing that your month can be filled with fun and interesting entries will lift your spirits. Once Carolyn knew where to look and had finished a little bit of work signing up, the opportunities just rolled in.

Then she went looking for a man.

What Carolyn did was to reverse the usual dating process: She built her list of enjoyable activities first, *then* she went looking for companions. When she had positive contact with a man online who seemed promising, she invited him to join her on an outing. It worked like magic! The man said "yes" and he was delighted to participate in a low risk, low expense activity planned by a woman he wanted to meet. If there was no chemistry, at least they both had an interesting time. If the first date turned out well, they arranged a second date without distractions so that they could concentrate on getting to know each other. Most often this meant going out to dinner and Carolyn was happy to explore the possibilities with a man she had already met.

This is what a successful series of first dates can look like when it's managed by a smart, resourceful woman. Carolyn had a wonderful time with the process and did, in the end, fall in love with a man she met online.

> *"It took a while to realize that Prince Charming was not going to ride over the Internet and ask me out to do the things I am interested in. My friends had talked about how disappointed they were with meeting men over coffee or drinks so I decided that I would see what else was possible. There are so many events and performances I was missing because I was too uncomfortable to go alone. It just seemed that combining first dates with my need for a companion was a perfect match!"*

How to build your social calendar: Resources for finding available activities

The activities available to you will depend on the area you live in. But I promise you that there are always more activities in your neighborhood than you would think at first glance.

Here are several places to start looking. It's good to sign up for email newsletters so you can have a steady stream of possible activities.

Local newspapers: All Sunday papers list activities. Not all are concerts with expensive tickets. Many are local organizations publicizing special events. This is a good way to find organizations which might otherwise fly beneath your radar. Check them out online. If they have a free email newsletter, sign up.

Schools: Are you near a college? If so, there are always concerts or lectures. Even the student theater performances can be appealing. Many of the larger universities have a "Critics Choice" weekly email that highlights a dozen or so activities on campus. You can sign up for this for free. Most events are free or cost very little. Didn't go to that school? It doesn't matter. As long as you are interested in life-long learning, you are always welcome on a college campus.

Film festivals or clubs: It's true that sitting in the dark watching a film won't give you any chance to talk, but if it's a film festival screening, it's more exciting than a typical movie at your metroplex. You'll be able to meet in the lobby before showtime. There are local film festivals with themes and inexpensive tickets. Even vintage films can be a lot of fun. If nothing else is available, you can always go see the latest blockbuster in 3D.

Art Museums: Joining your local museum is one of the best financial deals available for first dates. For an annual membership of $50 or so, you get to go for free any time during the year and the museum usually has members' only events about once a month. These can be wonderful evenings to offer for a first date. I am enthusiastically in favor of museum membership as a first dating tool, even for men who know nothing about art. As museums change exhibits, you'll have a never-ending variety of easy, free activities to offer a date.

Natural history and science museums: Every major city has an important natural history museum, but even smaller towns have visitor centers or animal rescue centers that make for an interesting tour. Personally, I love aquariums. If you're lucky enough to live near a major natural history museum, consider becoming a member as part of your dating project. If you feel a little intimated by art museums or worry that your date might feel intimidated, joining a natural history museum is a good choice.

Symphonies: Going to the symphony can be a pretty formal affair. I love going to hear classical music performed live and relish any opportunity to go to a concert. Even if you're not near a grand symphony hall or would really prefer a more casual venue, you'd be surprised by how many local classical music groups you can find. Churches and local universities have frequent concerts and tickets are inexpensive. Sometimes, even world-class symphonies will surprise you if you know how to get half-price tickets. (Register for free with www.goldstar.com.) If you love classical music, sign up for all the free newsletters you can find. You will know from a man's profile what kind of music he enjoys. Going to hear a musical performance is always a great choice for a first date.

Music clubs: Do you enjoy live music in small, casual settings? Folk, blues and jazz clubs these days have email newsletters with their current calendars. Most have inexpensive ticket prices. What's especially helpful is that tickets are almost always available for mid-week performances. Do you agree that a Wednesday night date feels much less pressured than a Saturday night date? If so, then going out to hear live music mid-week can be a great first date. Would you go to club all alone? I usually wouldn't. This is an excellent chance to do something you enjoy that you would hold back from doing if you didn't have a companion.

Sports teams: A ticket to the baseball or football game can be expensive, but if you know that you are both interested in sports, exploring your options here is made so much easier if you "go Dutch". Maybe you both enjoy watching tennis or college basketball. Do your first date while cheering on your favorite team.

Community centers: While most community centers specialize in classes, they sometimes have one-time events. This might be a holiday bazaar, a spring flower show or a great speaker. Schedules are usually offered quarterly.

Libraries and bookstores: Don't overlook what a resource your local library and independent bookstores can be. Seeing a visiting author can be memorable, and afterwards you can browse the shelves and compare notes. Larger libraries often have art or document exhibits that are worth a visit. And book sales are fun. You can hunt for treasures, laugh and splurge on books without breaking the bank.

Botanical gardens: What could be better for a spring date than a stroll in a public garden? You can join as a member and have a similar range of perks and opportunities as membership in a museum: free admission, a newsletter with events, plus a controlled environment with guards and docents. I recommend visiting a botanical garden on a warm weekend. Also, many universities have gardens you can visit that might not be so well publicized.

Special interest groups: This could be almost anything: a hiking club, a birding group, a cooking school, a wine-tasting club, a sustainable energy support group. Recently, I went to a lecture hosted by an electric car club. There were over a hundred people there listening to a speaker about electric car batteries! This is an example of a group you could easily not find unless you look in the announcement section of your local newspaper. If you have more than one printed paper, get all of them just one time and take a good look.

Search the web for "off-the-beaten-track" tours: There are entrepreneurs everywhere looking to organize off-beat and interesting activities. Want to spend an afternoon making cheese or sausage? How about a walking tour of an historical neighborhood? Most organizers have calendars posted online.

Meetup.com—The online special interest group site: Meetup is really wonderful—a gift to singles. Go to www.meetup.com to sign up. You will be offered a menu of interests to select. When Meetup groups in your interests are formed or when existing ones announce a new meeting, you will get an email alert. It's really a great service to find free or low-cost activities that are not advertised anywhere else. Meetup groups do everything from wine tasting to hiking to concerts to lessons on social media and blogging. If you don't find a Meetup group that suits you, you can form your own!

Public affairs forums: Most larger cities will have an organization dedicated to lectures from well-known authors, opinion leaders and visiting diplomats. In San Francisco, we are lucky to have two: The Commonwealth Club and the World Affairs Council. Go to Google and search for "Speaker Series" or "Public Affairs Forums" in your area. From reading the man's profile, you will have a good idea of his range of interests so don't be shy about suggesting that the two of you go hear a renowned speaker, instead of going for coffee. This will be well received, especially as you will offer to "go Dutch". Tickets are typically $10—$25.

Comedy Clubs: Visiting standup comedians can put on great shows and there's a comedian for every taste. If you have a local club, sign up on their email list. Sometimes music clubs have a Comedy Night.

Ask your friends and family: Newsletters and email lists are everywhere these days. Your friends may have suggestions on which ones are good to join. They may know church groups that offer interesting activities, or historical societies or model train collectors or dog show events that you would enjoy.

Enjoy creating possibilities: Try to cast your activity net as widely as possible. You are creating possibilities. Like the director of a movie, you want options! More options! You will edit later and decide what hits the cutting room floor. For now, be excited about building a social calendar and the opportunity to make your first dates as interesting as possible. Be optimistic and positive that you will have a great time... and you will!

STEP 10
CREATING ENJOYABLE
FIRST DATES

So many women report that their experience with first dates is lackluster, boring and unproductive. Are you one of them? If you've met several men online for first dates, are you usually disappointed and feel that you've wasted your time? You can change that starting now!

One of the primary reasons that so many first dates are mediocre is that very little thought or effort has been put into the activity. *"Let's meet for coffee"* may seem like a good idea because it's an easy choice and coffee shops are on every corner. It even seems like a small investment of time and money. But is a coffee first date really a small investment for you? You've put time into maintaining a profile and managing emails. You've researched the man and only agreed to meet him because you think he'll be an agreeable companion with potential for more. You've paid attention to what you're wearing and possibly moved something else off your schedule. You might even be excited and nervous.

What if the guy is a dud? You will have wasted all of this preparation on a cup of coffee. Some of us go on first date after first date, drinking cup after cup of coffee, wondering why we are wasting our time being disappointed.

You can fix that!

THE NO-FAIL EQUATION FOR ENJOYMENT

Start by recognizing that every first date has two components for success: the companion and the activity. It's an equation: The Man + The Activity = Your Outcome.

If you depend entirely on one component, the other doesn't matter. If the man rates 100% and having a non-memorable coffee rates 0% then you are depending entirely on the quality of the man's company for your time to be interesting and worthwhile.

Depending entirely on the man looks like this: 100% + 0% = 100%.

But what happens if the 100% man you hoped for turns out to be a zero?

0% + 0% = 0%. You have nothing.

Why do this to yourself?

The other way you can approach first dates is balance the importance of the companion and the activity. You've invested a lot of effort to find the companion. You've screened and researched the men.

Why not invest just a little additional effort to upgrade your activities and break the habit of being 100% dependent on the man's company for your good time? That way, if the man is a zero, your experience won't be a zero.

Try this equation: 75% interesting activity + 0% man = 75%

Better, right?

Nothing can shield you from disappointment if the guy doesn't work out, but if your first dates are based on interesting activities instead of just coffee, your view of the whole process will shift.

Here's how: your social life will be much more enjoyable. You will be experiencing events and activities that you wouldn't do alone. You'll have dates and still have the opportunity to meet Mr. Right. When it's not Mr. Right, your time will *still* be interesting because you weren't depending 100% on the man. Over the weeks and months of dating, your social calendar will fill with concerts and plays and exhibits and festivals and events of your choice. Your memories of dating will be pleasant and happy instead of a string of boring disappointments. You will feel active and empowered. You will be upgrading your social life.

You will have fun!

What's the secret? Taking the initiative to suggest interesting activities for your first dates and offering to "go Dutch."

Enjoyable activities don't need to be expensive, and in the 21st century, there's no reason why a woman shouldn't offer to pay her own expenses. Don't pay for his. Just pay for your own. If you prepare a go-to list of activities that you enjoy and can afford, then you can take control of suggesting where to meet. You'll be amazed at how many men will be happy and relieved to break the coffee habit.

I'm going to walk you through every step. There are sample emails to help you, plenty of tips and a clear list of safety rules. There's a lot of material in this chapter that will shake up your thinking about first dates. Feel free to jump around. Just be sure that you read all sections. Read on and enjoy!

INVESTING IN YOUR GOOD TIME

Let's talk about money first: What if you were to invest $10 or $20 towards having a good time on each first date?

Have you considered a monthly entertainment budget? It's fair to say that you will not be able to mount an active dating life without incurring some costs. Even if you have very little to spend, you will still have a much more enjoyable time on first dates if you suggest activities which genuinely interest you and then offer to pay your own way.

Reducing dates to meeting for coffee is a form of risk management for most men. It's a way of minimizing costs while maximizing exposure to as many women as possible. The man you're going to meet expects to meet several other women as well as you, and if he is responsible for paying for everyone all the time, he's going to keep his first dates as inexpensive as possible. But 99% of men will jump at the chance to do something more creative if they feel that the financial arrangements are fair.

Here are some comments I heard when I offered to pay my own expenses on a first date:

"When I read the words 'go Dutch' it was the key to the door! I'm so pleased to be going to the concert with you. Thank you!"

"Thank you for your generous offer. Why don't I get the theater tickets and you buy us drinks before?"

"Great idea! Let's meet in the lobby at 6:00."

Let's take a look at how little it actually costs to go out and have a worthwhile first date if you take a little trouble to plan ahead and prepare a go-to list of activities:

- Coffee might cost $5, but for $15 you could have an evening out at a museum where you are dressed nicely, look great and have an interesting time even if the guy doesn't send off sparks.

- For $20, you could go to an experimental theater performance that might be hilariously funny or deeply poignant...and have an interesting time even if the sparks don't fly with your date.

- For $25, you can go to an independent film festival event worthy of discussion, be relaxed and learn something about film art...and have an interesting time even if the sparks don't fly with your date.

- For $30, you can go to your local blues or jazz club to hear a great show and have a drink…and have an interesting time even if the sparks don't fly with your date.

- For $35, you can go out dinner then see the latest 3D blockbuster at your local metroplex…and have an interesting time even if the sparks don't fly with your date.

- For $40, you can go to an upscale wine and cheese tasting and join a trendy and witty crowd…and have an interesting time even if the sparks don't fly with your date.

- For $50, you could get a half-price ticket to the symphony, dress up in your best night out clothes, and enjoy inspiring music…and have an interesting time even if the sparks don't fly with your date.

You get the idea! For more suggested activities see Step 9: Getting Ready to Date for a list of resources.

You've offered "going Dutch" but the man still wants to pay

It's simple: say *"Yes, thank you!"* Some men, particularly older men, have a firm identity as the provider and are genuinely uncomfortable with a woman paying her own way. If your goal is to see that both of you have a good time and are comfortable with each other, do what makes him comfortable. Don't bicker about this or go back and forth until the payment is an awkward moment. Be gracious and let him pay if he prefers it.

Why it's absolutely fine for a 21st Century woman to pay her own expenses

We've all heard about *"The Rules"*. If you look online for commentary on whether the man should pay for the first date, you'll inevitably find strong opinions that state *"Absolutely, he should pay."* Usually, this advice is aimed at younger women who are hoping to meet their first husband.

The topic of women and money is broad and complex. It really deserves a book of its own since the scope of the issues is beyond what a book on online dating can realistically cover. What I can offer here are my opinions based on my own life experiences as a woman over forty who is dating again in the 21st Century.

Money is power. If we are worried about the Glass Ceiling and women being advanced in positions of corporate and political power, how is it not backwards to insist that a woman must be passive and depend on a man to provide all the money for dating? As someone who spent her career as an entrepreneur and CEO, I find it insulting for a dating advisor to tell me that I need to depend on a man to whip out a $20 bill in order for me to have a good time and also have the potential of a relationship with him. If the man really wants to pay, he should be allowed to, but I think it's silly to be afraid of a woman paying her own way on a first date.

Defining what is "appropriate behavior" for men and women is a major challenge of our times. Technology is dissolving traditional means of communication. Women are being educated and entering the workforce in record numbers. For women over forty, our worldview is different than that of a twenty-two year old just starting out. We have mature careers. We manage people, run companies and manage households. We are smart and capable. And experienced! We've paid car loans, mortgages, health insurance, filed tax returns, probably managed a divorce, possibly handled teenagers and have had to make many hard choices over the years.

So, after all of that, do you really want to insist that a man must pay for 100% of your date knowing that this will doom you to endless cups of coffee? Insisting that he must pay for everything is a nineteenth century social tradition designed to make women behave "appropriately" because men had all the financial power. This seems so out of touch today! When we have earned our own money and are willing to invest in ourselves, it's foolish to limit planning our first dates so only the man pays. If we do that, we insist on maintaining 19th Century traditions of male and female inequality.

With our decades of experience, women over forty can reinvent how we date. Our mothers and grandmothers faced enormous social pressures about their roles with money. We don't have to be passive or go back there. We don't need to limit our potential for quality experiences based on archaic social rules. Today, we can make it easy and forward facing: just say "Let's go Dutch!"

DON'T JUST HAVE COFFEE! CHOOSING AN INTERESTING ACTIVITY IS SO MUCH BETTER

When you take control of choosing what to do on a first date, you protect yourself from feeling discouraged and disappointed. You know that you'll be doing something enjoyable that you want to do, with the added bonus of meeting a new man.

Maybe your date will lead to something romantic and wonderful. Maybe it won't. But you can guarantee that you'll have a good time if you take control. Don't just depend on the quality of his company. Consider your experience as the sum of _all_ the parts: the activity, your investment of time and money _and_ the potential to meet a wonderful man.

Making the activity your primary source of enjoyment is an approach to online dating that requires new thinking. We have been so programmed by marketing departments to think that all we need to do is lay eyes on someone and bells will ring. But the truth is that you will probably meet a lot of men without a single ding-dong ringing anywhere. So, what's the best way to guarantee that you don't waste your time and get discouraged?

Take control.

It does take courage. Know that you can do this! Your life will be so much more interesting and full for making the effort.

Our culture still expects that the man will ask first and the woman should be passive. When we were in high school, this felt like the natural order. I would have been terrified to call a boy first! Now that we're over forty and with so many of us running our own businesses, being managers or working in positions of leadership and responsibility, waiting for the man to make the first move feels a little childish.

I confess, I do like it when a desirable man asks me out. But, with online dating, he most often is going to ask for coffee to hold the financial costs down over multiple dates. Remember, if the man does all the asking and all the paying, he can run up considerable expenses and be pretty tired! Virtually all of the men I dated were so relieved that someone else stepped forward to make suggestions.

The quality of his time counts, too. Men get just as bored and disappointed going out for coffee. You can read in the message boards how stung some men feel taking women for dinner if they are just used as a meal ticket. It's legitimate that men have concerns about how to invest dating time and money. They don't want to be used and they don't want to waste their resources any more than you do.

Be imaginative. Be creative. Be courageous. Take control.

Finding Activities and How to Use a Social Calendar

How will you know what to suggest for your first dates? You may already have weeks full of social activities and know that building a social calendar is part of a balanced life. Some of the rest of us aren't sure where to start. We work, we keep households running and many of us take care of children or elderly parents. Some of us are so busy with day-to-day tasks that we're lucky to go to the movies with a girlfriend and call that our social life.

For those busy women without a social calendar, now that you've decided to date, it's worth investing just a little time to see what events and activities are happening in your area. If you live in a large city, this job is easy! If you're in the suburbs or rural areas, you will have to subscribe to email newsletters or print newspapers to stay current with what's offered. Wherever you live, there are interesting things to do that will enrich your life.

The decision to date is a clear choice that you are ready to reinvent yourself and your lifestyle. Doing interesting things is a big part of this but it does take a bit of planning to know what's available so you are not caught by surprise. Remember, one of the best practices for having enjoyable first dates is to avoid last minute scrambles!

Can you commit fifteen minutes a week to researching things to do for the next thirty days? You can keep track of potential activities with this simple method:

- Get a paper calendar (or use an online calendar if you're more comfortable).

- Every time you hear about something interesting, mark it down. This will become your personal "go-to" reference file for dating activities.

- Note whether you have RSVP'd or bought a ticket.

This does not need to be an overwhelming project but it is important that you stay current with your social options. You don't want to sit home alone with nothing to do, right?

Planning ahead is covered more extensively in the chapter *Step 9: Getting Ready to Date*. You will also find a list of *10 Great Activities for First Dates* in *Part Two* of this book. If you want to consistently have a good time on your first dates, read these chapters and get ready to upgrade from *"Let's meet for coffee."*

165

Don't forget the equation: 0% + 0% = 0%. Your time is valuable. Make an investment by planning to make your dating hours more enjoyable.

Choose Activities That Will Flatter You

What on earth can that title mean: *"Choose activities that will flatter you?"* It's simple, really. Chose activities for your first dates that will feature you in your most flattering setting, in your best looking clothes and that let your personality shine.

I look great in a little black dress or a dark suit. Classic, I know, but reliably flattering. That's why for my first dates, I usually offered activities that involved a little dressing up: museum visits, classical music concerts or art gallery openings. For all of these, a little black dress, good coat and colorful scarf were a reliable uniform that I could wear to give me confidence, knowing that I looked good and was dressed perfectly for the activity.

Since I'm in my sixties and my legs haven't aged well, I avoided first date activities that called for wearing shorts. I've had those varicose veins treated twice, but they've come back and still make blue lines on my legs. Later, when the man wants to look deeply into my eyes, I won't care about how my legs look, but on the first date, it matters to me.

Is this all about appearance? You bet it is. I want to feel good and look as good as I can. If I know some outfits or settings aren't going to flatter me, they are not on my go-to list for first dates. Examples would be going to a pool or beach, which I enjoy, but want to save the bathing suit exposure for a later date.

My knowledge base is particularly strong with art and music and pathetically weak with sports. You have probably gathered by now that I tend to go for art and music venues for first dates. I'm also very interested in travel and the history of other cultures, so exhibits from around the world in museums or local universities are solid choices for me. If I chose wisely, the event will be interesting, I'll sound and look good and have a fine time even if the man is not a keeper.

Don't "test out" a new activity for a first date. Choose a venue that you know and enjoy. Choose an activity that is familiar so that you are relaxed and don't have unnecessary surprises. Let the man be your only surprise. Hopefully he's a pleasant one.

SAMPLE EMAIL INVITATIONS

Here are eight sample emails that suggest meeting for the first time as well as offer choices of activities you and your date will both enjoy. You can easily see that these samples follow a pattern that you can copy.

My advice is to keep this email invitation short and to the point. The offer of meeting is a big step for some people. For others, it's relaxed and natural, especially if they've had a lot of experience with online dating. If you're new, and it he's new, it's better to keep this email very simple and clearly organized. Let the information about activity suggestions be the focus and avoid adding anything extra.

Your choices of invitation should be determined by what you have read in his profile. It's not hard to find a man's interests. Presumably, you would not be having continued contact with him unless you have some of those interests in common.

How many emails should you exchange before you're wondering about meeting the man? I would say no more than three. You should have a pretty good idea after three emails about whether you want to continue or pull the plug. If you vote is to "continue," why delay? It's just a practical choice to find out about the chemistry sooner rather than later. Do you really want to dilly-dally around online when you could see the guy in the flesh? No! If you're sincere about wanting to meet a man and getting away from your computer and into a more interesting life, ask to meet him.

How quickly this kind of email goes together depends on how you've kept up with news about local activities. As we will discuss in the chapter on *10 Great Activities for First Dates*, planning ahead by signing up for email newsletters from activity groups and generally paying attention to what's happening in your area will save you from scrambling at the last minute. If you always have a "wish list" of activities you'd love to do, it only takes a few minutes to put them in an email.

Choose the opening sentence you like best, plug in your choice of activity and you're ready to go!

Here are email samples you can use as models:

Dear Jeff,

Thanks for the email! I'm enjoying our correspondence but, in all frankness, I'm not a fan of long-term emailing. I'd rather meet sooner rather than later and see what happens. Do you agree?

Let's choose an activity we both enjoy. I'm happy to "go Dutch" and pay my own expenses so it's fair and comfortable for you. It will also be more interesting than meeting for coffee, as much as I love a good cappuccino!

Here are a couple of choices:

Thursday, March 21, 7:00 pm: Classical guitar concert at Morgan Hall. We could meet in the lobby at 6:30 and chat. Tickets are $20. Here's the link: www.morganhall. org/events/1248

Tuesday, March 26, 6:30 pm: Member's open house at the Modern Art Museum. Always a lively time. Free. I have a membership and can bring a guest. Here's the link: www.sfmoma.org

If either of these work for you or if there's something else you're interested in, just let me know. After you decide, it will be easy to figure out the logistics about how to buy tickets. I'll meet you in the lobby. Just look for the blue scarf and a smile!

Looking forward to meeting you,

Christie

Here's a sample email invitation for a theater and art lover:

Dear Steve,

Thanks for the email! Would you like to meet?

I hope you are interested in doing one of these activities. We could just go for coffee but I'd prefer to do something we would both enjoy and am happy to "go Dutch" and pay my own expenses. Since we both like to go out for theater and art, this seems like a better plan to make an interesting time together instead of just another coffee date.

Here's what caught my attention:

Wednesday, April 24, 7:00 pm: Repertory Theater Company does the comedy "Button Our Toes." Tickets are $24. Here's the link: www.RTC.org

Saturday, April 27, 10:30 am: Wine and Art Festival at Comstock Park. Free. Here's the link: www.wineandart. com

Anything else you suggest would be welcomed! After you choose, we can figure out the details. It will be easy to meet at the entrance. Just look for the red scarf and a smile!

Looking forward to meeting you,
Christie

Here's a sample email invitation for a sports fan:

Dear Pat,

I'm enjoying our emails. But...I have to say that I'm not a fan of long-term email correspondence. Would you like to meet?

I would love to go to a baseball or basketball game with you since we are both fans and I'm happy to "go Dutch." It's fair and I'm comfortable with paying my own expenses. I hope you are comfortable, too.

Let's choose a game! Here are some times that work for me:

Thursday, April 18, 7:00 pm
Friday, April 19, 7:00 pm
Sunday, April 21, 2:00 pm
Wednesday, April 24, 7:00pm
Saturday, April 27, 2:00 pm

We could buy tickets in advance or at the gate. Sometimes, Craigslist has good tickets for sale. After you pick a time, we can figure out the details.

Looking forward to meeting you,

Christie

Here's a sample email invitation for a nature lover:

Dear David,

I'm enjoying our emails, but honestly, I'm not a fan of email correspondence that goes on for weeks. Do you agree?

Would you like to meet? There are several interesting activities coming up soon that would be a good first meeting. Let's "go Dutch." That's fair and I'm happy to pay my own way.

Since we both love being outdoors, how about one of these choices:

Tuesday, May 14, 6:00 pm: Hiking Club sunset walk around the lake. Meet the hike leader at the boathouse. Small fee. Here's the link: www.hikingclub.org

Saturday, May 18, 10:00 pm: Botanical Garden Open House. Docent tours every hour. Entrance fee $15. Here's the link: www.botanicalgardentours.org

Sunday, May 19, 1:00 pm: Bird watching at Audubon Canyon. Let's go see the herons nesting. Guided tours every hour. Entrance fee $20. Here's the link: www.heronnest.com

We can meet at the entrance and just pay the fees there. I'll be easy to find. Just look for a yellow hat and a smile.

If there's anything else this month that you'd prefer, just let me know. The weather is gorgeous!

Looking forward to meeting you,

Christie

Here's a sample email invitation for a movie fan:

Hi Will,

Thanks for the email! I'd be interested in meeting you if you'd like to move forward. I hope you do.

Since you're a movie fan, can we find a film that would be a good choice? We could meet in the theater lobby 30 minutes before and chat a bit. I'm happy to "go Dutch" and buy my own ticket.

Here's what might be interesting:

Wednesday, June 12, 7:00 pm: The Independent Film Festival has a showing of "Beyond All Measure" at the Metro. I love this old, classic art deco theater. Here's the link: www.indiefilmfestival.org

Friday, June 14, 7:00 pm: Let's pick a blockbuster at the local metroplex. I like science fiction but am flexible.

Tuesday, June 18, 7:00 pm: The Museum of Modern Art has a showing of classic film noir along with a lecture. This would be my first choice! Here's the link: www. sfmoma.org

If there's another event which looks more interesting to you, just let me know. I can meet you in the lobby. I'll be easy to find. Just look for the blue scarf and the smile!

Looking forward to meeting you,

Christie

Here's a sample email invitation for an active athlete:

Dear Barry,

Thanks for the email! I'm so pleased that you love to play tennis, too. Would you like to meet for a volley and friendly game?

There are public courts at Dunsmuir Park. We should be able to get a court right away or not have to wait too long. I'll bring a bucket of tennis balls and a smile.

Here are some times that are good for me:

Tuesday, July 9, 7:00 pm: It's the end of the day but still good sunlight.

Saturday, July 13, 10:00 pm: Prime time at the courts but we can chat while we wait.

Also, if you have any interest in going to the tournament next weekend, we could look at getting tickets. I'm happy to "go Dutch" and pay my own way. We may only be able to get nose-bleed seats but I would love to see Roger Federer play.

Let me know if any of these choices look good to you. If we want to get tickets, we can work out the details later.

Best,

Christie

Here's a sample email invitation for a gardener:

Dear Jerry,

Thanks for your email. I love roses, too.

Would you be interested in meeting at the Rose Garden for a quick walk through the blooms? If we're inspired, we can go on to Orchard Nursery and take a look at their selection. I have a place for three new bushes, plus it's just fun to look at a beautiful garden center in full summer splendor.

Here are some times that work for me:

Wednesday, July 24, 5:30 pm: The Rose Garden is open until 7:00 pm that night.

Sunday, July 28, 3:30 pm: We could catch both the Rose Garden and Orchard.

If you have a favorite gardening book, please bring it! We can work out the details when we pick a time but I'll be easy to find. Just look for the green scarf and a smile.

Looking forward to meeting you,

Christie

Here's a sample email invitation for a man who loves to cook:

Hi Jack,

Thanks for the emails. I'm enjoying our correspondence. Would you like to meet? I hope you don't think it's too

*forward of me to ask, but I'm not a fan of long, protract-
ed email exchanges. Let's see what happens next!*

*Since we both love to cook, I have these suggestions. For
anything with a fee, I'm happy to "go Dutch" and pay
my own way.*

*Wednesday, August 14, 6:00 pm: The author of a real-
ly interesting new cookbook will be speaking at Kitchen
Goods in the Stanford Plaza. Italian Farm Cooking.
I'd love to hear her. There will be food samples. Free but
we need to reserve places. Here's the link: www.kitchen-
goods.com*

*Saturday, August 17, 11:00 am: Thai food cooking class
at the community center. There are spaces available if we
act fast. $40 each and includes all ingredients that we'll
eat for lunch. The class is 2 hours. Here's the link: www.
awcommunitycenter.org*

*Tuesday, August 20, 6:30 pm: Bookstore Browse. Let's
visit the large Barnes and Noble and browse their cookbook section. We can share our favorite titles. I'll bring
my favorite recipe if you bring yours!*

*If none of these work for you, I'm open to any other
"Foodie" suggestion!*

*Looking forward to meeting you,
Christie*

ENDING THE FIRST DATE: HOW TO HANDLE THE "SHALL WE MEET AGAIN?" QUESTION

Near the end of every first date there is an awkward moment
when the question *"Shall we meet again"* comes out in the
open for discussion. You and he are considering this privately
all along, of course. Usually, it's better to let your time together

flow without the interruption of making public judgments until the last possible minute.

So, just know that this is a really awkward moment. With all my years of business experience, hiring and firing people, giving sales presentations and being rejected many times, I still find the statements at the end of a first date to be very uncomfortable, even if you like the guy and feel certain that he likes you, too.

You can only control 50% of the response to your date. It's especially awkward if you like him but he doesn't want to see you again. So sorry! If any reader knows some good lines or has suggestions on how to make the *"Judgment: Should We Meet Again"* discussion less awkward, please let me know!

But, it must be done.

You may find that the man jumps the gun, thanks you for the evening and says that *"We're not a fit."* If so, shake his hand, thank him in return and wish him the best of luck. Remind yourself that there are literally *"More where he came from."* Plenty more. You will meet other men, have good first dates, enjoy yourself and move forward into the future.

Do not try to negotiate if the man is declining future contact. Remember that men are just as sensitive about stalkers as women. Don't be weird. Just absorb the news, put on your best professional behavior and thank him for the time. In this respect, a first date is something like a job interview.

If possible, it's much better if you take the lead and indicate your thoughts first. It takes an act of courage, especially if you're not sure what the man is thinking. Towards the end of the date, turn on your radar for a good moment to bring up the topic of "What to do in the future."

You will have drawn one of three conclusions as your time together has progressed: 1) You don't want to see him again; 2) You are not sure and might be willing to see him again;

3) You are enthusiastic and hope he is, too!

Here's what to say if you are sure that you don't want to see him again:

"I'd like to check in with you about our date. Thank you for the lovely evening! I really appreciate meeting you, but I suspect that we're not a fit and my guess is that you feel the same way, too."

Here's what to say if you are not sure and might be willing to see him again:

"Can we check in about our date? How are you doing?"

Then, depending on his response, you can say *"yes"* or *"no"* to another date. If he's also unsure, suggest that you get together again and see where it goes from there.

Here's what to say if you are sure that you want to see him again:

"I've had a really good time with you. Can we check in about whether we're going to see each other again? I would like to. What are you thinking?"

Or:

"Thank you for the lovely evening. I've had a very good time and would be interested in seeing what happens if we continue. What are you thinking?"

And, by the way, congratulations! I hope that this promising first date leads to many wonderful choices in your life!

Is being "Activity Partners" a fourth option? Can you convert a decent guy who's good company but not a romantic prospect into a friend?

"Activity Partner" means that you've converted a first date from a potential romance into a platonic friend who shares a strong interest. The two of you can go together to events with no expectations of romance.

This is a wild card and it's hard to pull off. After many, many dates, I've only been able to make this happen with one man.

I met John, my only activity partner conversion success, on a first date. He was great company but neither of us could explain why there was no chemistry. There just wasn't. We both love small, live theater productions and often struggle to find someone to go with. I approached him with this:

"I really like you and we both have flexible schedules. I'm always struggling to find someone to go see theater on weeknights. You go often. I'd love to be one of your activity partners and be able to go to the theater with you! It's not going to work out as a romance between us, but it would be wonderful to have you in my life. Would you be willing to give that a try or, at least, think about it?"

I said that, or variations on those words, to three wonderful men, all smart, talented, interesting guys whom I would have loved to have as friends. Two rejected me outright. One of them said *"No, I can't do that. I want more."*

Fair enough.

Some men don't have any experience being "just friends" with a sexually active, available woman. It's easy to see how this could make a guy who is searching for a girlfriend really uncomfortable because being an activity partner would be a constant reminder of being rejected. John was exceptional in that he could handle the sexual rejection while appreciating the friendship. Plus, he had plenty of other first dates so the pressure was off me very soon!

BE SAFE!
SEVEN COMMONSENSE RULES
OF PERSONAL SAFETY

If you are going out to meet strangers, you can never be reminded too many times about the basic rules of personal safety. You've heard these before. Make sure that you follow them.

Here are the basic safety rules for meeting strangers on first dates. We covered the safety rules for setting up your profile and protecting your identity in previous chapters.

Rule #1: Never agree to meet a man until you have researched him

If you're serious about meeting a good man online, you can never be too busy to spend ten minutes checking him out. Plus, since *he* knows that *you* know his name, career and connections, this will go a long way towards making sure that this stranger doesn't make stupid mistakes.

Please remember that 99.9% of the over-forty men online are decent, reasonable guys who are looking for serious relationships. (At least once you've weeded out the married men by doing your research.) If they could be accused of anything, it's probably that they're socially awkward bumblers. Your biggest worry will most likely be that the guy will be dull, with no chemistry and bad table manners. Try not to obsess about possible axe murderers.

Rule #2: Always let someone know where you are going and whom you will be meeting

Be sure that you leave your schedule, destination and the ID of your first date companion with a trusted party. Text or email your itinerary to a friend, or, if you have roommates, leave the information in a note on the kitchen counter. Include your estimated finish time so you can text/call to take the person "off duty."

Rule #3: Handle your own transportation going to and leaving the date

Never violate this rule no matter how bad the weather is, or how slow public transportation is running. Take your own car or make your own arrangements. Do not accept a ride home. If it's offered, decline politely.

Rule #4: Meet in a public place

Since you are following the *Hopeful Woman's Guide* and have chosen an interesting activity for your first date, this won't be a problem. I like to meet in the lobbies of museums and hotels because the light is flattering!

Rule #5: Leave from a public place

It's a good rule to make a clean parting in a public place, but occasionally I have accepted an escort back to my car or to the train station. Given that the man knows my name by now, seeing my car license number hasn't been an issue for me. Please use your own judgment about this rule. It's more flexible than the others.

Rule #6: Use good manners: End the evening graciously, even if you don't want to meet the man again

Take the high road, no matter what you think about the man. Say "Thank you very much for making the effort to come out and meet. I'd like to wish you the best of luck."

Rule #7: Don't break the safety rules!

PART TWO

HELPFUL REFERENCE LISTS

Select the Most Promising Men
With the 12 Question Score Card,
Great First Date Activities and
Knowing Your Must-Haves
and Deal Breakers

THE
HOPEFUL WOMAN

THE 12 QUESTION SCORE CARD

A QUICK CHECKLIST TO HELP YOU DECIDE WHETHER YOU WANT TO CONTINUE WITH A MAN

Some women are very methodical and like to keep track of the men they are meeting online with notes and spreadsheets. Are you one of them? I find spreadsheets to be excessive, but I do like to keep notes. You may find a helpful way to keep your notes organized is to have a checklist.

When you first launch your profile onto a dating site, it will be a busy time for you. Most sites have a way of flagging new profiles so lots of men will visit and look at what you've published. This can be a very productive time to meet men, but it can also be a challenge to keep the guys sorted into those you'd like to explore further and those you'd like to delete.

One practical way to keep track of which men you'd like to meet sometime soon is to use this *12 Question Score Card*. For each positive answer to a question, the man scores one point. If he doesn't score at least ten positive points, you need to extract yourself and start again with another man.

There are twelve sample questions below but feel free to write your own. Just be sure to have at least twelve questions to give the man a fair chance. Any one negative answer could be a deal-breaker—see the chapter on *Know Your List of Potential Deal-Breakers*—or you could choose to judge the man by his grand total.

Some of my friends were worried that if they eliminated too many man there wouldn't be others to go out with. The trick here is to find a balance. You want your judgment to be fair to the men and you want to be respectful of your time and not waste your energies corresponding or meeting men who are obviously not potential candidates to help you achieve your dating goals. It might be a good idea to review the section on understanding your goals in the chapter *Step 1: Getting Ready.*

Keep score by adding one point for each question you can answer with "yes".

Circle each "yes" or "no" answer:

Question#1: Appearance: Did you like his picture? Does he seem appealing? Can you envision yourself standing next to him?	**Yes**	**No**
Question #2: Communication: Can he communicate clearly? Is his grammar and spelling acceptable?	**Yes**	**No**
Question #3: Does he seem interesting instead of boring? Do the descriptions of his interests and activities indicate a zest for life?	**Yes**	**No**
Question #4: Interests in common? Do you share some of his interests or see yourself learning about them? Do his interests excite you?	**Yes**	**No**

	Yes	No
Question #5: Politics and religion? Are his political and religious views comfortable for you?	Yes	No
Question#6: Education and achievement? Does he match you in levels of education and accomplishment? If he doesn't, are there other factors which make this less important? Is he more educated and accomplished than you? Is this comfortable for you?	Yes	No
Question #7: Optimism? Does he seem to be upbeat and optimistic about his future?	Yes	No
Question #8: Relationship goals? Does he express the same goals as yours in his search for a relationship?	Yes	No
Question #9: Negativity about past relationships? Is his profile free of complaints about previous relationships or about negative experiences with women in general?	Yes	No
Question #10: Respect for you? Have all of his contacts with you been well-mannered and respectful?	Yes	No
Question #11: Does He show genuine signs of interest? Has he read your profile and made interesting comments on your content? Has he been attentive to subject matter in your email exchanges?	Yes	No

Question #12: Does he work to build your trust?	Yes	No
Has he agreed without protest to provide you with his name and links to confirm his identity? Note that a refusal here is a deal-breaker and invalidates all other points!		

GRAND TOTALS: YES ____   NO____

Did he pass? Congratulations on finding a man with great potential!

If you are considering meeting a man who has scored at least ten "yes" answers, be sure to do your research about him. Then take the initiative to suggest that you meet while doing an activity which you will both enjoy. (See sample invitations in *Step 10: Creating Enjoyable First Dates.*)

Best wishes for an enjoyable first date and a happy future!

10 GREAT ACTIVITIES FOR A FIRST DATE

You have read the chapter *Step 10: Creating Enjoyable First Dates* and you have learned the No-Fail Equation for Enjoyment. For readers who skipped ahead, let me just repeat the equation briefly:

Recognize that every first date with a new man has two components for success:

the companion and the activity. It's an equation: The Man + The Activity = Your Outcome.

Depending entirely on one component means the other doesn't matter. If the man rates 100% and neither one of you have put any effort into the activity, then you are depending entirely on the quality of his company for the quality of your time.

Depending entirely on the man looks like this: 100% + 0% = 100%.

But what happens if the 100% man you hoped for turns out to be a zero?

0% + 0% = 0%. You have nothing.

Let's be realistic about finding a bell-ringer on your first coffee date. Or even your tenth coffee date. It could happen, but we're not high school kids who live in a fantasy world anymore. Our lives are more complicated and we should be able to be more practical and realistic. Plus, we want and deserve to have a worthwhile experience whenever we to go out and socialize. We can go out for coffee with a girlfriend.

Let's upgrade our dates! We want memorable, high-quality hours for our efforts. Let's do something fun and interesting!

The practical way to approach first dating is to balance the importance of the companion with the activity. You've invested a lot of effort to find the companion. You've screened and researched the men. *Why not invest just a little additional effort to upgrade your activities and break the habit of being 100% dependent on the man's company for your good time?* That way, if the man is a zero, your experience won't be a zero.

Try this equation:

75% interesting activity + 0% man = 75%

This is so much better!

Consider what you could look back on after six months of online dating experience: companionship for a series of interesting activities you enjoyed, or, six months of meeting at Starbucks. Each timeline offers you the chance to meet men, but only one gives you the guarantee of months of interesting activities to build good memories on and an optimistic attitude about future dates.

It's an act of self-respect to say, *"My time really matters!"* For more details on how to find activities and suggest them to the men you meet online, see the section on building a social calendar in *Step 9: Getting Ready to Date*. The sample email invitations are in the chapter *Step 10: Creating Enjoyable First Dates*.

THE 3 GOLDEN RULES FOR PLANNING HIGH-QUALITY FIRST DATES

Dating Golden Rule #1: Chose an interesting activity that you enjoy but might resist doing if you didn't have a companion. Forget going for coffee. It's boring!

Dating Golden Rule #2: Offer to "go Dutch." Freeing the man from paying for everything on your first date creates so many upgraded activity opportunities. It's only fair that you do your part to contribute to the first date before you know each other. Plus, offering to "go Dutch" gives you control over the activity selection.

Dating Golden Rule #3: Take the initiative! Offer a choice of two or three activities for the first date. Be flexible and agreeable to whichever one he wants. Most men will be thrilled that a wonderful woman has taken the time and trouble to find something fun to do and then takes the initiative to invite him to join her. Really. Men are delighted and taking this approach completely separates you from the crowd. You will establish yourself as creative and an enjoyable companion.

THE 10 GREAT ACTIVITIES FOR FIRST DATES

Try to have a list of no less than ten possible activities for first dates. That way, you'll never feel pinched or be caught unprepared. You will always be able to offer your date at least two choices.

What follows is the list that I put together for myself. You can use this as your starting point. Edit this list to fit your own interests and to match what's available in your area.

1. Meet at a bookstore:

This is a step up from going for coffee. It's low-risk and low-investment but still interesting. You can browse the books together and have plenty of conversation topics easily presented to you. If the meeting is going well, you can always go to dinner after the bookstore.

2. Meet in the lobby of a local museum:

This is my personal favorite. Museums have so much to offer and are beautifully designed environments. You can dress up and look your best if you choose an art museum. Even if you know very little about art, you will find an exhibit that will stimulate conversation. No advance ticket purchase is required. You can buy tickets when you arrive at the front desk, or go when the museum is free—usually one evening a week or one weekend day per month.

If you are a museum member, you can attend evening events that are like glamorous, exclusive parties with beautiful lighting, no-host bars and crowds of people whose excitement is contagious.

Not an art museum fan? No problem! Go to a natural history museum or planetarium instead. Museums are centers of the community. Check them out!

3. Meet at a music club:

I love doing this for a first date because I'm shy about going into music clubs alone. Find the folk club, jazz club, rock club, blues club or country and western club in your area. There's so much music to enjoy! Meet in the lobby or at the front door. Tickets are usually around $20. If it's a popular place, decide ahead of time who will purchase the tickets.

I have bought the tickets often and have <u>never been stood up</u>. My date always showed up on time and paid me back.

4. Meet at a local theater for a performance:

This is another favorite of mine. I love going to the theater for big Broadway shows (these tickets can get pricey) or small, intimate local theater groups. The local group tickets are often very reasonable and many shows can be found on www. goldstar.com at half-price. Meet in the lobby. If your email exchange has been especially promising, you might meet for a light dinner before the show.

5. Find an event at your local college and meet on campus:

All schools have programs which feature performances from traveling musicians and dance troupes. The performances cover a wide range of interests. Plus, there are often presentations and lectures which are open to the public. You can learn more about science, travel destinations, anthropology and so much more. Be a life-long learner and take advantage of your local college. They usually have a free newsletter. Sign up!

6. Go to a local sporting event:

Like basketball, baseball, football or tennis? Game tickets might be expensive and it might seem like a long time to be together with a first date, but if you're seriously interested in the guy and you are both sports fans, pick a game and figure out via email how to buy the tickets. Where I live, college basketball and football are economical choices and fun. Meet at the sporting arena.

7. Go to a festival:

In the spring or summer, you can find street fairs almost every weekend. Events with great food carts and plenty of free music make for a happy stroll. And, it's usually free! You can sit down at a cafe to get out of the crowd. (OK, it's like going for coffee but with benefits!) Enjoy a brief visit at the festival or linger if your date is going well. Just don't forget to arrive and leave separately.

8. Go to a wine and cheese tasting:

There are so many places to find wine tastings. Perhaps you have a local winery that will do a tour or you can find a club with private tastings (check out www.meetup.com for wine tasting clubs). Galleries and wine merchants also host events. There are Wine and Cheese Festivals, often at harvest time at the end of summer. From elegant to casual, wine tastings can give your first date a sophisticated focus. If you don't drink wine, watch for chocolate tastings. Yum!

9. Meet at an antique car show:

I can't resist these since I love classic cars. Mentioning this in my profile drew several men with a similar interest. There is usually an admission fee at car shows but then you have the chance to walk through a fascinating cross-section of history. If cars aren't your thing, how about boats? Or airplanes? The title could have been "Meet at a Vehicle Show". How about a ride on an antique train? If you live in a city with a museum for science and technology, these often include user-friendly exhibits that you will enjoy with your date.

10. Classical music is romantic. Meet for a concert:

Going to the symphony is another opportunity for an elegant evening. Most symphony halls are lovely places to meet for the first time when both of you are looking your best and the music is stunning. Tickets can be expensive so make your arrangements carefully and check www.goldstar.com for half-price tickets.

Chamber music concerts are often in more intimate settings with inexpensive tickets, so check your local listings for recitals. If you enjoy vocal music, there are many choral performances ranging from church concerts to your local college choir. If you both love to sing, invite him to a sing-a-long!

Personally tested for a good time

I have tried each of these ten activities for first dates and all of them have been fun and interesting, even when the man wasn't a "keeper." I ended up having a steady stream of companions because I had done my online homework by researching the man's interests and matching them up with activities I wanted to do, too. I was able to enjoy going to the theater, concerts, museum openings, music clubs, symphonies and wine tastings—most of which I would not have done alone.

When the man was interesting, I was grateful. It was easy to pay attention to him and schedule a second date (usually a dinner date) where we could concentrate on getting to know each other. If he wasn't second date material, I was still grateful to have had a companion to do something enjoyable.

Remember: When you are meeting a stream of men over the internet you should protect yourself from wasting your time on boring and disappointing coffee dates by taking the initiative to create interesting activities for your first dates. You will then be able to look back over your dating experiences with pleasure. And, while you're having a good time doing a variety of enjoyable activities, you are also setting yourself up to meet a wonderful man. You'll be relaxed and ready.

Enjoy yourself and good luck!

DEFINING YOUR RELATIONSHIP MUST-HAVES and DEAL-BREAKERS

It's worth taking a few minutes to make some notes on what you truly want to create in a relationship. It will help you be more confident and clear-sighted when you read a man's profile.

Most of us <u>think</u> we know what we want, but we haven't taken the time to really make a list of what is essential for us to have in a successful relationship. The result is that we often get involved with men who can't satisfy our needs. We wind up disappointed and move on to the next experience. Sometimes we learn from our mistakes instinctively. Sometimes we just repeat the same errors over and over again.

Now that you've decided to meet a new man, it's worth taking some time to consider your "must-haves" and "deal-breakers" in a relationship. Whether you find a man online or in some other way, knowing these will keep you from looking at inappropriate men and may potentially save you a lot of heartbreak.

The checklist below is a way to start thinking about what's essential for you to create in a new relationship. It's a starter list for your reference. You should feel free to eliminate statements from this list and add your own.

Start by deciding which of these statements ring true for you. Not everything will, but when one does, take note of it. The flip-side will be your deal-breaker. For example: I want a smoke-free and drug-free life, therefore smoking or using drugs is a deal-breaker for me.

Health, Diet, Exercise and Attitude:

- I want to be with a man who doesn't smoke.

- I want to be with a man who doesn't use drugs.

- I care about eating a healthy diet with fresh foods.

- I'm a vegetarian and my mate must be a vegetarian or vegan also.

- I don't drink very much and don't want to be with a man who drinks more than socially. Heavy drinking is a deal-breaker for me.

- I lead an active lifestyle with a priority for exercise. I can't be with a man who is out of shape and won't make changes to get healthy.

- Anger management is critical to my mental health. I don't want a man with a temper he can't control. Any physical or verbal abuse is completely unacceptable.

- I can be supportive of a chronic illness (ex: diabetes, hypertension) but cannot be supportive of destructive behavior. I won't be with a man who is not open about any health issues and not actively working to improve his health.

- I believe I have the power to make positive differences in my life. I am optimistic and believe the future is hopeful. The man in my life should be an optimist, too. Pessimism and negativity is a deal-breaker for me.

- I have a sense of adventure and love exploring new places. I am not phobic about flying. Not being willing or able to travel is a deal-breaker for me.

- I am a homebody and am happy surrounded by what's familiar to me. Being asked to leave home constantly is a deal-breaker for me.

Geography:

- I like where I live and don't want to move to a different area. The need to relocate would be a deal-breaker for me.
- I am flexible about where I live and don't mind moving to accommodate a new relationship.

Education, Politics, Religion and Money:

- I am curious about the world we live in and I am committed to life-long learning. I don't wish to be with a man who is closed-minded or refuses to learn new things.
- I appreciate good English grammar. It would be hard for me to spend time with someone who doesn't speak or write well.
- My religion is important and I need a man who shares my faith.
- My political beliefs are important and I need a man who agrees with my politics.
- I'm nervous about having enough money and scraping by month after month. I prefer that a man have a steady source of income. If a man can't hold a steady job, this is a deal-breaker for me.
- I do not wish to financially support the man in my life. I want financial partnership. I expect to work to help support our lifestyle and expect that he will also contribute financially.
- I am excited by entrepreneurship. I run my own company or want to start one. I need a man who can tolerate the ups and downs that come with being self-employed.

- I expect to be financially supported by the man in my life. Not being supported is a deal-breaker for me.

Personal Appearance and Housekeeping:

- Appearance matters to me. A man who's a slob and wears dirty clothes is not a good match for me.

- Personal hygiene is important to me. I don't want to be with a man who can't bathe or groom to my standards.

- I want to be with a man who has good table manners. I don't want to see chewing with an open mouth.

- Good housekeeping matters to me. It's important to me that a man knows how to keep his home neat and clean.

Sex and Monogamy:

- Being active sexually is important to me. I enjoy sex and want to be with a man who is a skilled and experienced partner.

- I am indifferent to sex and would prefer not to have an active sex life.

- I believe that being faithful is essential to a relationship. I can't tolerate my partner having a sexual relationship with anyone else.

- I don't insist on an exclusive sexual relationship with my partner and expect to have the same freedom for myself.

Family Life:

- My children are the most important part of my life and any relationship with a new man would have to come second to the needs of my children.

- I have no children now but am very much hoping to have children in my future. A man must want to start a family for me to start a relationship with him.

- My children are grown and I don't wish to start again with young children. A man with young children is not for me.

- I prefer a child-free life. I am not interested in having children or being a stepmother.

- I'm close with my family (parents, brothers, sisters) and expect a new man to be willing to spend time with my family.

- I expect to be respectful and supportive of the needs of a new man's family, especially if he's caring for elderly parents.

PART THREE

BONUS CHAPTERS

Straight Talk About Monogamy,
Sex, Body Size and Money

WHAT IF HE IS STILL MARRIED?

A WORD ABOUT MONOGAMY

The status of being part of a couple can be quite nuanced these days but, in my mind, there is still one iron-clad rule:

If you are married or in a committed relationship and your spouse/life partner believes that both of you are monogamous, then YOU HAVE NO BUSINESS DATING OTHER PEOPLE.

If you are a married and reading this book for tips on how to date someone else but your wife or husband doesn't know your plans, close the book right now and GET OUT OF HERE! I am writing for consenting adults whose life choices are out in the open. There will be no sneaking around, cheating, philandering or advice on how to lead secret lives here.

OK. Let us assume that everyone here is freely available.

Separation and divorce are complicated transitions, especially when there are children or money involved. There are also husbands whose wives have long-term, debilitating illnesses and they have "an arrangement."

In my experience, most men with "arrangements" about postponing their divorces for any reason do not write about this in their profiles but prefer to tell you in person. This is another strong point for meeting the man sooner rather than later! (See *Step 9 Getting Ready to Date.*) Usually, in a quiet moment over a drink or meal, an honorable man will roll out His Position Paper. Or, this would be the opportunity to roll out yours if you are the one with the unusual situation.

To continue seeing someone under the pretense that he or you are unencumbered with legal or other obligations is both deceitful and cruel. My advice is to tell the truth as soon as you can.

If you hear an unusual story, you will have to check with your conscience and judge your comfort level. Try to imagine that you are in each of the other positions. What if you were his wife? What if you were him? If you can honestly say that you feel no conflicts or that your actions will not harm anyone if you continue dating a man in this position (and if you believe the story he's telling you) then let your conscience be your guide.

"But I love him. I want to be with him!" My friend, Allison, fell in love with Will, who was still married but living separately. Will and his wife had decided to not divorce until their children left for college, two years in the future. Will had his own apartment and was also a devoted, attentive father. It was awkward for Allison, who was divorced with grown children, but she was so smitten with him that she decided to see where the romance would go. This story has a rare but happy ending. After several months of dating, Will and Allison moved in together. Openly. When Will's youngest child left for college, his divorce proceeded. At some point, Allison and Will may decide to get married, but the most important thing for her is that her conscience is clear.

What about the money? Divorce is expensive in so many ways. Money is often the reason divorce doesn't happen, especially in a community property state like California. We've all heard that ugly, jokey phrase *"it's cheaper to keep her."* These days, with almost half of working wives earning more money than their husbands, you could also say *"it's cheaper to keep him."*

Kathy had a promising date with a man working in Silicon Valley, land of computer millionaires, so she was surprised when he said *"We just couldn't afford two places, so when my wife and I separated, I moved into the guest room."* He didn't have a plan— the separation was brand new. Kathy wisely decided that this was too complicated for her and wished him good luck and good-bye.

When you start dating online, you will run across men who are still married but hope to find another relationship. With any luck, you will meet men who are honorable and honest about their circumstances so you can make an informed decision. But, just in case, TURN YOUR RADAR ON HIGH ALERT. Pay attention to any clue that he has misrepresented his divorced status.

I was tricked by a married man myself, and was already on my fourth date with him before I saw a pattern in his behavior. Dan had put up a profile on JDate which said "Divorced." He was quite wonderful and I was interested. Our first date was an early Thursday evening dinner. Then he cancelled our Saturday night date at the last minute with profuse apologies. Two other midweek dates went well but it was followed by another weekend cancellation. Hmmmmm...? I called a friend who is a divorce attorney and she ran a search for me about divorce filings and found nothing in the nine surrounding counties. The next time he called, I asked him directly, and he confessed that his wife had early Alzheimer's. Dating was part of how he was coping.

Sad, I know, but not for me. No thank you. No liars.

If you have any experience with a married man who is representing himself as "Single" or "Divorced" online, do not hesitate to flag his profile and report him to the site's management.

Here's a shocker: my neighbor's husband went on OKCupid and contacted me. *Definitely* my neighbor's husband. No, he did not recognize my profile picture. But, I recognized his.

"We have so many interests in common," he wrote.

I wrote back, careful to not reveal my name, but identified his house, his pets...*and his wife...*and insisted that he get off a site for singles immediately. The next day, his profile was gone. Thank goodness. And no, I never told his wife.

So, to wrap this up:

- Be honest and honorable.

- Tell no lies.

- Don't waste your time with liars.

- If the marital situation is unusual, make an informed decision.

- Try to keep things simple. Isn't your life complicated enough?

A FEW WORDS ABOUT SAFE SEX

We live in the age of Herpes and HIV. Maybe it's been a while since you've been sexually active and it seems like a difficult and frightening new landscape out there, filled with new risks. I was sealed up in a twenty-six year marriage that started before the AIDS epidemic and before Herpes was as widespread in the US population as it is now. I was terrified of sexually transmitted diseases (STDs) when I started dating again. So if you feel uncomfortable about this, believe me, I know your pain!

There are limits to answers that books can give you. Please check with your doctor for up-to-date medical knowledge about STDs and the best current advice for practicing safe sex.

One of the best online sources of information about STDs is the website from our national Centers for Disease Control and Prevention (CDC). It's a well-organized resource with up-to-date answers to frequently asked questions on all STDs. You can also enter your zip code and find testing locations in your area.

Go to: http://hivtest.cdc.gov/STDTesting.aspx

Insist that he get tested before you have sex with him

Tests for STDs are easy to find, inexpensive and should be mandatory for any new sexual partner you choose. You don't know where he's been! If he's not worried about the results, he shouldn't resist getting tested. If he is worried about the results, you should be, too. You should want to know exactly what is going on.

Get tested yourself

Your sexual partner has every right to be just as careful as you are. It's a myth that men are so driven to have sex that they will ignore everything in the pursuit of getting laid.

Once, I was in a romantic position, kissing with a delightful man in front of a beautiful fireplace. It was our third date, and everything seemed so right. Then suddenly, he sat up straight and clutched both my shoulders, turning me so I faced him directly.

"Do you have herpes?" he demanded. *"Do you have HIV, have you ever been exposed? Have you been diagnosed with chlamydia?*

I shook my head as he continued. *"What about gonorrhea? Syphilis? Genital warts?"*

By the time he worked his way down the list to crabs, I was definitely out of the mood and somewhat shell-shocked. Gee, no one could fault him for wanting to know, but he could have picked a more gracious way of bringing up the subject of STDs.

Why don't you take control and set the mood? Don't wait until the last minute when both of you are panting, stripping off your clothes and already in the act. Be practical. There will never be a totally comfortable time to bring up this awkward topic, but you can make the best of it by being gracious, considerate and matter-of-fact. It's a discussion you should have for your safety, whether you want to or not. Just do it.

So, what if you have herpes. When should you tell him?

If you have genital herpes, you are not alone. The CDC states that one out of every six people between ages of fourteen and forty-nine have the infection. Officially, it's known as the herpes simplex virus type 1 (HSV-1) or type 2 (HSV-2). You or your sexual partner might not even know that you carry the genital or oral herpes virus because many people have no symptoms.

If you are certain that you have herpes, you should be responsible about not spreading it. If you don't know and there might be ANY chance that you have been exposed, you should get tested.

Telling a potential sexual partner that you have genital herpes surely must be one of the most awkward tasks a responsible adult can do. It takes a lot of courage and character to be truthful AHEAD OF TIME so your partner can make an informed choice: either to go ahead and have sex with you with adequate protection, or to abstain from having sex with you.

There is a risk. You could certainly lose your chance to have that man as a lover after you tell him. But if the two of you are sufficiently attracted and already feeling bonds of attachment, there is hope that you can figure it out. With so many millions of adults carrying genital herpes, rest assured that there are plenty of couples who can make their relationships work.

It's when new partners are not told the truth that real problems arise.

"He never said anything!" My friend, Clare, moaned after her doctor confirmed that the sores in her genitals were herpes. *"He should have told me. I love him and I'm willing to figure out how to deal with this. But he didn't warn me and we had unprotected sex. I feel so betrayed."*

What Clare's boyfriend did was completely unfair and dishonest. He let her believe that they could have risk-free, unprotected sex. What a louse. He took advantage of her trust by never bringing up the subject of STDs until it was too late.

Clare was too inexperienced and naive to ask. (This was a long time ago, before awareness of STDs was so widespread. But the man certainly knew that he had herpes.) When she was angry and confronted him, he said that he had been too scared to tell her. Fortunately, Clare wound up as one of those lucky cases who rarely have outbreaks. She went on to marry that man and have children with him. Later, he also betrayed her about money when he was too scared to tell her that he'd lost his job and walked off with her money. Maybe she should have been more alert about his character.

After she divorced, Clare remembered her anger and swore that she would never take advantage of someone's trust. Now, she is one of many single women who ALWAYS make sure that a frank and open discussion about STDs is a major part of moving a relationship forward. Sure, sometimes it stops the movement cold, but Clare knows that she has been safe, honorable and trustworthy.

Or...it could turn out that he has herpes, too! Julia was head over heels for Eric. They were moving rapidly towards getting physical. With her heart in her throat, Julia pulled a condom out of her purse and opened the conversation by saying, *"I need to tell you why we have to use this. I'm so sorry to tell you this but you need to know that I have herpes."*

Eric threw back his head and laughed with relief. *"So do I! And thank you for telling me so soon."* He went on to say that it just made him trust her more. He was impressed with her courage in taking the first step to tell him. When I last heard from her, she and Eric were still a couple, happy and building a life together based on love and trust.

If he hadn't had herpes, they could have figured out what it takes to keep a relationship going. As you can see from the next story, it's definitely possible to maintain a sexual relationship even if one partner tests positive while the other tests negative.

MaryAnn has herpes and has been seriously dating a man who doesn't. They are both in their sixties, so having children is no longer an issue. Their sex life is completely normal except for these four things they do to keep him herpes-free:

- MaryAnn washes her genitals with soap and water carefully before they make love.

- Her boyfriend always wears a condom.

- After they finish, he washes his hands carefully with soap and sometimes with hydrogen peroxide which they can buy off the shelf at any pharmacy.

- When she has an outbreak, she takes medication prescribed by her doctor. They wait until the outbreak is completely over to resume physical contact.

Two years later, their relationship is healthy and happy. They are planning to move in together. If anything, knowing that she has been responsible and trustworthy from Day One has only brought him closer. And...they have a satisfying sex life.

So, what's the message here for you? It's simple to say but hard to do: Be brave. Be honorable. Be trustworthy. You may lose a date but you will gain self-respect. You know what it takes to do the right thing: Start the conversation about STDs. Ask him. If you have an STD, tell him about it sooner rather than later.

Always use a condom with a new lover

"Don't be silly: cover your Willie." My sons and I used to make up little jingles like that when they were teenagers and I was trying my best to program them to always use a condom. Of course they were horribly embarrassed but I didn't care. Their safety was my primary concern.

Your safety should always be your primary concern. Yes, your pleasure is important and pleasing the man is also important, but make sure that you aren't making any mistakes tonight that you will regret tomorrow.

See that he wears the condom.

In my world, this is non-negotiable. If you are firm in your position and present it in a matter-of-fact tone, you should not have an argument. If he argues, give some serious consideration to what this says about his character. Could a man who ignores your safety be someone who can make your happy in the long run? Probably not.

Carry fresh condoms in your purse. Do not rely on the man to have a supply, although most will. If you bring your own, you will know about the freshness and the quality. Do not let him talk you out of using a condom for any reason. Some men, particularly older men, worry that they will lose their erection if they use a condom. OK. So what? Better he should lose his erection and you have to look for alternatives to pleasure each other than you taking any risks with STDs.

So, how do you bring the condom up (if you'll forgive the pun) assuming that he doesn't already have one in his hand? Try these statements:

"I have condoms in my purse."

"Would you like me to put it on you?"

"Which color condom would you like? I have red and blue."

"Do you need a latex-free condom?"

Please check with your doctor about which activities require condoms. Intercourse, of course. Some doctors recommend condoms for oral sex. You should gather all the current information you can and make an informed choice that will result in your safety. I am not a doctor nor is anything written in this book meant to be any substitute for qualified medical advice.

Stay informed and stay safe!

BODY SIZE:

WHAT IF YOU ARE OVERWEIGHT?

First, let me prove to you that I truly understand people who struggle with extra weight. In 1995, at the pinnacle of my pre-divorce-marriage-misery, I topped the scales at two hundred and fifteen pounds.

These days, I'm divorced and weigh between one forty-five and one fifty. I am a size ten and work hard to stay in shape. Successfully losing weight and keeping it off took a solid, long-term commitment from me to modify my behavior. It took a lot of discipline. I was also very lucky to be able to get help in the form of hypnosis therapy and personal trainers. (Both of which I recommend very highly if you can afford it.) On top of wanting to look good, I had a general terror of having a stroke or heart attack and dying young because I was morbidly obese. And, finally, I was lonely and didn't want to deal with any push-back about fat and attractiveness issues in my future dating life.

But this is not a book about weight loss. It's a book about how to generate enjoyable first dates with online profiles and how to have a good time going on first dates until you meet a man who lights up your heart.

So, what if you are overweight? I mean not just a little which you can hide by wearing black clothing and encasing yourself in Spanx. No, I mean carrying enough extra pounds to give you a BMI of over thirty which labels you in the medically obese range.

BMI stands for "Body Mass Index." You find it by first knowing your weight and height. The formula is weight (pounds) divided by the square of height (inches), then multiplied by 703. A "normal" weight BMI range is between eighteen and twenty-five. You can find the definition and charts on Wikipedia.

Let me tell you about my friend, Anne. Not long ago, I was on a holiday weekend trip with two single women in their fifties. Both are recently divorced. One woman, Marcia, is slightly plump but not overly out of shape. The other woman, Anne, is smart, creative and charming, and her body shape is what my mother used to call "a butter ball." She is round. No amount of black velvet can cover the reality of her rolls of fat on her tummy, the backs of her arms and around her hips. Her eyes sparkle and her personality shines but the simple truth is that she is fat and badly out of shape.

We were visiting and catching up and I told them about the *Hopeful Woman* book I was writing. Anne pounced on me for dating advice but I couldn't bring myself to tell her my true opinions about her weight issues. I like her and didn't want to hurt her feelings. So, by the error of omission, I did her a disservice by completely avoiding any mention of her weight and appearance. I was trying to be kind but, in the end, I'm not sure that it was helpful to pretend that her obesity doesn't exist.

Please forgive me if you find the following comments painful, but here's what I should have told my friend, Anne:

There is a difference between being overweight at twenty and being overweight when you are over forty.

Young women are justifiably irritated if all a man cares about is a slender appearance. For someone in her twenties who is very healthy in general, a few extra pounds shouldn't be a deal breaker. But, by the time we reach forty, those few extra pounds may have grown into a good-sized load.

Please note that I'm not talking about ten or fifteen pounds. American women are slammed continually with negative feedback about our bodies. If you are only a few pounds over your ideal weight, you can stop reading this section on fat and stop worrying now!

But, if you are a heavy older women with a BMI of thirty or more, you should know that with online dating, your appearance raises these additional burdens:

Legitimate health concerns: What about high blood pressure, heart disease and diabetes? Obese people in their forties without any signs of high blood pressure, high cholesterol and high blood sugar are indeed fortunate. Most medical professionals would say that if your BMI is over thirty, you are at risk. So, whether you have already developed significant health issues or whether you are at risk, a sensible man has to wonder what the consequences would be for him.

Questions of self-control: Being able to control yourself is a primary indicator of what it's going to be like to live with you. If you can't control your overeating, what does this mean for other areas in your life?

Questions of self-management: Living a healthy lifestyle is a top priority for many smart, achieving men. Or even men who just want to live long lives! Your weight is evidence that you do not share these values. You can say that you do, but being obese contradicts this. It's the old cliché of "actions speak louder than words." If you overeat and don't exercise properly, you are much less likely to be able to attract a man who is committed to being fit. Even a man who is out of shape himself may not want the negative reinforcement of being around someone who demonstrates poor health habits.

These are harsh words and I am sorry to speak so bluntly but there is no point in trying to sugarcoat this. If you are seriously overweight, you will significantly diminish the number of men you will be able to attract online.

And, it would be unfair to accuse these older guys of only caring about appearance. They're not teenagers. Since they're over forty, they are dealing with their own health realities. Some of them are widowers and don't want to take undue risks in losing another wife prematurely so they will select for the healthiest women they can find. This isn't unfair. This is survival, plain and simple. Others with teenage daughters may be looking for women who can be positive role models.

The truth is that it's just easier to meet men online if your weight is not an issue. Please don't fall into the trap thinking that all men over forty are looking for bikini-perfect twenty-five year olds and that's why they are not responding to your profile. I swear to you from my own personal experience that this is not the usually the case. There are plenty of men who are realistic about meeting women their own age. But, you are shooting yourself in the foot with most of them if you have packed a lot of extra fat onto your body and aren't actively working to get yourself fit.

You can do something about it! I lost over sixty pounds and kept it off. If you are determined to change your life, you can, too.

There is help available to you when you are ready to commit to get fit. I tried Weight Watchers and found going once a week to be very helpful. Exercise, of course, is a must, as is portion control. For that, I highly recommend hypnosis therapy for help with self-control and cravings. (I became an unabashed fan of hypnosis when it helped my mother quit smoking after she chain-smoked for forty years. Google "hypnosis for weight loss" to find a hypnosis therapist in your area.)

Best of luck to you and don't be discouraged! Committing to love and take care of yourself is a first essential step in finding a loving relationship.

DON'T GET CHEATED!

HOW TO AVOID SCAMS AND CON ARTISTS

It didn't take con artists and scam artists long to notice that millions of women were searching for love online. Most of us are too sensible to be hooked in by a man with a wild, implausible story of temporary hardship. Unfortunately, there are vulnerable, trusting women who don't know any better and get cheated and conned.

Don't be one of them.

Advice for keeping yourself safe from scam artists is pretty simple: do your research about what a man says is his situation, especially if he doesn't live nearby and can't meet you. So many thieves take advantage of the fears women have of meeting strangers online. They assume that a shy, lonely woman would want to have a long email correspondence. They work their way into offering emotional support and virtual companionship.

And then, there's a crisis and the man needs money. Just for a short while. He's stranded in Indonesia on a business trip because the flights to Hong Kong were cancelled. His charge cards don't work. Can you wire him $1,500 just until he gets home then he'll pay you right back? Or, oh my God, his sister needs emergency surgery and she doesn't have health insurance so everyone is donating to help her. She'll die unless we all help! Please, please send $3,000. Or, this is terrible and he's sorry to ask, but his car just died and he needs it to get to work. He has a big commission check coming at the end of the month. You're his best friend! He loves you! Could you help out with a temporary loan of $5,000 just for two weeks? Of course he commission can easily cover this and more. Maybe he can fly out to meet you and hold you in his arms at last?

What stories! Were you ever working in an office that received faxes from Nigeria from a member of the royal family? In my office in the late 1990's, we used to receive these faxes about once a week. It was always some very highly placed official in a dictatorship government who needed to get money out of the country and wanted to transfer $100,000 into our account. We could keep $25,000 for our trouble. Just send him the account numbers. The stories were so outrageous that we couldn't understand how anyone would fall for them.

But people did.

It happens all the time: women fall for stories from men who want to take their money. It's so sad. Hearts are broken when these sweet, innocent women discover that the man who has been emailing them so lovingly was really just a thief. Please, keep yourself safe and don't fall prey to a long distance email romance with requests for money.

Wise women follow a simple rule: It doesn't matter how much he says he loves you, never send money to a man you've never met. Never. NEVER.

ABOUT THE AUTHOR

Christie Jordan has spent her career as a product designer, brand manager and entrepreneur, inventing and launching products sold through retailers including the Home Shopping Network, J.C.Penney, Macy's, Bloomingdale's, Disney and The Home Depot. Becoming single after a long marriage led her to explore online dating and to write a focused, realistic guide for other single women over forty. Christie studied at the University of California, Berkeley, and the Harvard Business School. She has two sons and lives in the San Francisco Bay Area.

Contact Christie at www.HopefulWoman.com

THE
HOPEFUL WOMAN
www.HopefulWoman.com

INDEX